THE TEMPLE
OF THE SPIRIT

By Francis Meehan

LIVING UPSTAIRS
THE TEMPLE OF THE SPIRIT

THE TEMPLE
OF THE SPIRIT

By

FRANCIS MEEHAN

E. P. DUTTON & CO., INC

NEW YORK · 1948

Motionless resting on the lake awhile,
   I saw its marge of snow-bright mountains rear
Their peaks aloft, I saw each radiant isle,
   And in the midst, afar, even like a sphere
   Hung in one hollow sky, did there appear
The Temple of the Spirit . . .

SHELLEY: *The Revolt of Islam,* XII, xli.

FOREWORD

Not by bread alone doth man live. That belief assumes that man lives on two planes, in two worlds, the material and the spiritual. He is acting on the material plane when he eats his dinner; on the spiritual plane when he enjoys the frescoes in the Sistine Chapel. I have used the term spiritual in its widest meaning; it includes all nonmaterial values.

I am far from maintaining that all spiritual values are of equal importance. But it is obvious that religion, literature, the arts and philosophy, because of their nonmaterial nature, content and scope, have certain elements in common. Historically, too, they have been interrelated, philosophy affecting religious belief and practice, the arts finding in philosophy and religion incentives and inspirations.

It is a sound theological position that the sacraments are efficacious according to the personal dispositions of the recipient of them. The man who goes through the marriage ceremony without knowing what he is doing or with the intention of not receiving the sacrament is not really married at all. His personal dispositions are negative.

Similarly, a poem or a piece of music is efficacious according to the personal dispositions of the reader or hearer. Our understanding and enjoyment of it, our vital assimilation of it, are conditioned by what we know and feel, and especially by what we are. Training, temperament, life experience, intellectual and emotional background all contribute to the quality of our response to a theory of existence or a masterpiece of literature.

Hence it is that a man's character—the totality of his habits of thinking, feeling and willing—helps or hinders his approach to things spiritual. Is he proud, stubborn, narrowminded; or is he humble, receptive, generous? Is he crippled by prejudices and irrational fixations? Is he capable of shedding opinions and beliefs when faced with proof that such opinions and beliefs are untenable?

Through fertile centuries the basic function of what were called the humanities, or the humane studies, was to aid the student to develop a personal background suitable for the recognition and appreciation of spiritual values. Those studies offered him knowledge and skill, standards and enthusiasms. He learned to know what was excellent and to love it, to make it a part of his life. The process involved a discipline that enabled him to make himself over; its effects disclosed themselves in his manners, his tone of voice, his conduct and his conceptions of happiness.

Some elements of that traditional discipline are restated in this book. They are not outmoded or outgrown. Rather it might be said that modern man stands in acute need of their assistance, for modern man is often confused and even overwhelmed by his helplessness in the spiritual world. Like Theseus in the labyrinth, he needs the thread of Ariadne to guide him through the confusions and complexities of these our dissonant days.

F. M.

CONTENTS

Foreword

CONTENTS

THE TEMPLE
OF THE SPIRIT

I NOT MADE WITH HANDS

THROUGH nearly four hundred well-wrought pages Mr. John P. Marquand records in *So Little Time* a modern saga of futility and frustration. His Jeffrey Wilson is a likable man, but baffled and myopic. To him the times are out of joint, as times always are for the rootless mind, however radical, and the restless heart, however kind. Jeffrey feels weary and ineffectual; the red apple of life has turned to ashes in his mouth. But he is no shallow self-deceiver, no apostle of facile uplift with an oily smile, a brilliantine animation and a home-made explanation of the cosmos. He has at least, and it is much, the saving virtue of humility.

As the novel ends, Jeffrey slips into Saint Patrick's Cathedral on New York's Fifth Avenue. Why, he isn't sure; but "above all he felt an impulse to be where it was quiet. It seemed to him that there had been too much travel, too much talk, too much noise for a long time, too much of everything. Inside Saint Patrick's he might be quiet for a few minutes, absolutely quiet." *

Once, years before, Jeffrey and his wife Madge had persuaded the sacristan to let them visit the Cathedral of Chartres by moonlight. They had held hands and said nothing and felt out of the world. Now in the American cathedral, in spite of his small-town prejudices and suspicions, he was aware of something "which had also been in Chartres, and he remembered what it had been. There was no sense of time. Although the scent of incense and the burning wax from all the candles spoke of time, still time did not disturb him."

Time is thus mastered by the watcher on some silent bastion of the timeless. Strong souls have learned, often after breasting turbulent waters, to shun enslavement by the spirit of their day; to turn, Ulysses-like, from the discordant music of the passing moment. They look before and after.

Mr. J. Donald Adams, a literary commentator rich in knowledge of the significant past and consequently impressive when he essays prophecy, has engaged in some searching speculations on the literature of tomorrow. In the vogue of such works as *The Robe, The Keys of the Kingdom* and *The Song of Bernadette,* he discerns a freshened interest in spiritual interpretations of character, life and history, and concludes that the torrent of cynicism and disillusion which succeeded World War I will not be duplicated in the years directly ahead of us:

> When we observe the presence of a succession of novels dealing with a religious theme at the top of the best-seller lists, it does not necessarily mean that we are to be deluged with more books of that kind. But the response to those books surely does indicate a widespread state of mind in which people are reaching out for positive values. They are tired of being told that there is nothing in which to believe; they are tired of reading

stories over-populated by subnormal and degenerate characters. They know that man is as capable today as he was in the
Stone Age of stupidity, baseness and brutality, but they are
also aware of the intelligence, courage and nobility of which
he is capable. This belief in man, this belief in the life that
can be, will be increasingly reflected, I think, in the shape of
books to come.[1]

Everywhere thoughtful men and women are looking for-
ward to what romantics and cynics call a brave new world.
Their sons have died that such a world might come to birth.
Even when dismissed as starry-eyed idealists, many of our
publicists and politicians, reflecting the sentiments and aspirations of the inarticulate masses, envisage better living
conditions in every land, the elimination of cutthroat competition and of racial and religious intolerance, the reign of
brotherhood and mutual understanding among classes and
nations, a chicken in every pot and a daily quart of milk for
every peasant and a radio choice of Sinatra or Shostakovich
on pleasant Sunday afternoons:

> There where the Ganges and other gees wander,
> And uncles and antelopes act for the best.

But how can such dreams come true? Our most realistic
thinkers know that laws, cartels, trade pacts, charters formulated by politicians at sea and benevolent compulsion of
the lesser breeds into democratic patterns of living will of
themselves and by themselves bring neither peace on earth
nor good will to men. They know that for all its practical

[1] *New York Times Book Review,* October 24, 1943.

15

value the science of economics can effect no basic or permanent rejuvenation of human nature. They know that plastics and jet planes will neither insure nor assure our deepest happiness. They agree with Willa Cather's sad-eyed scholar in *The Professor's House* that at its constructive best science has done nothing but make us very comfortable and at its destructive worst very insecure. They endorse the belief of Mr. Maxwell Anderson:

> If the time arrives when our young men and women lose their extravagant faith in the dollar and turn to the arts we may then become a great nation, nurturing great artists of our own, proud of our own culture and unified by that culture into a civilization worthy of our unique place on this rich and lucky continent between its protecting seas.[2]

They discern that the golden age we all so passionately desire will depend on the degree to which individual men and women the world over recognize, reverence and actively cultivate those positive values called the imponderables.

Rightly are spiritual values so called, for literally they cannot be weighed; nor can they be analyzed in a test tube, studied under a microscope; neither can a price be placed upon their head:

> Nor is there any comparison between the good that a man may do to his fellows by teaching them sound business principles (if business has principles), and on the other hand by teaching them something of the spirit and what it has seen on the way. The upholders of the first kind of work always win

[2] Address at Carnegie Institute, October 14, 1937.

16

their shallow arguments by showing precisely in pounds, shillings and pence just what is the gain to man, while the upholders of the other kind know that here is a value that pounds and shillings and pence are all three of them equally unable to estimate. We do not even know the price of a dawn.[3]

Imponderable is the price of a dawn, and imponderable are Ravel's "Bolero" and Donatello's "Faun," Wordsworth's "There Was a Boy" and Giotto's "Lily of Florence blossoming in stone," the *Meditations* of Marcus Aurelius and the *Autobiography* of Saint Teresa. Imponderable are art, music, sculpture, architecture, literature, philosophy, religion. Yet they are the necessary, the satisfying, the abiding things, for they are the things of the spirit. To finite existence they give an infinite meaning. Our world planners labor in vain if they leave the imponderables out of account:

> What is a man,
> If his chief good and market of his time
> Be but to sleep and feed? A beast, no more.
> Sure, he that made us with such large discourse,
> Looking before and after, gave us not
> That capability and god-like reason
> To fust in us unused.[4]

Radio commercials blare unctuous warnings against our deficiency of Vitamin B. Through all the centuries of our cumulative human wisdom the ablest thinkers have stressed our deficiency of spiritual vitamins, the values whereby we

[3] Lord Dunsany: *My Ireland* (Tauchnitz Edition), pp. 9-10.
[4] Shakespeare: *Hamlet*, IV, 4.

17

live as befits human beings. "Law shields society from the violence of brute force," says Dr. Henry J. Bigelow of Harvard, "but no law protects it against the encroachment of brute intellect." Spiritual values, which alone differentiate Plato from the ape, must of necessity mold the shape of books to come, the shape of life to come. Divorced from the imponderables, education is superficial and impotent, government is hypocritical and vain, civilization itself is a menace and a blasphemy.

The traditional classification of the imponderables into philosophy, religion and the arts recognizes in each a specialization of function and a distinctive sphere of influence, and implies a hierarchy of spiritual values; but in all of them and in each of them spiritual values inhere. Music is no substitute for metaphysics, and metaphysics is no substitute for poetry; the head cannot say to the hand, I have no need of thee. Each has its unique importance, its own aims, ideals, techniques, standards and preferences; likewise its own prejudices, blind spots and limitations. It is natural, perhaps inevitable, that the devotee of music or philosophy or religion should exalt and magnify his chosen approach to truth, happiness and inner satisfaction by minimizing and depreciating other ways that lead to ultimate wisdom. Priest and prophet, monk and minstrel have rarely seen eye to eye. Yet, as has been finely said, "Truth is a summit, and every path that goeth upward leads to truth."

Because they all lead upward, because they open vistas on spiritual reality, the imponderables have much in common. Some holy men have become poets, and some poets have become saints. He who toils at the oars and he who strums a guitar are both in the same boat. Baudelaire and James Joyce were obsessed with religion, even if in reverse; and Ernest Dowson and Huysmans sang themselves to their knees.

Plenty of men, often intelligent, less often intellectual, doubt or deny, in whole or in part, the reality of the imponderables. They are indifferent to the Dutch masters, unmoved by Beethoven's Seventh Symphony, unimpressed by the Taj Mahal or Bernini's colonnade, and at mention of Aristotle or Abélard, Kant or Croce, they cry out with impetuous young Romeo, "Hang up philosophy!" More commonly they are impervious to the evidences in the field of religious thought, history and experience. A few of them even draw the reckless and readily refuted conclusion that anybody who professes belief in God, Revelation and the immortal soul must be either a dolt or charlatan, the victim or the instrument of clerical craft.

All the arguments for and against spiritual values have been formulated in books, sometimes eminently readable, sometimes more conducive to heat than to light. Those books, for the imponderables or against them, have made converts, but for the most part they serve to fortify the already existing faith or unfaith of their readers. The warfare they engage in is unending, and victory is never unequivocally decisive. Always there will be a Lucretius and a Lucian, a Volney and an Ingersoll, and always a Saint Paul and a Plotinus, a Pascal and a C. S. Lewis.

More reasonably persuasive, surely, are those thinkers and teachers whose aim, in Gilbert Murray's words, is less to convert than to contribute. They inspire us to reflect calmly and objectively on the functions and effects of the imponderables in modern life. Aloof from the controversialist's lust of battle and the missionary's single-purposed zeal, it is possible and profitable to study the imponderables, to recognize their role in complete living, to indicate some of the time-tested ways whereby their potentialities may be realized and the horizon of the human spirit enlarged. Even the least sympathetic reader will concede that the imponderables are at least worth looking into; only the fool hath said—in his heart and in his haste—There is no God.

In our day and in our world countless men and women like Jeffrey Wilson vaguely experience intimations of immortality. They feel "that hungering after the ideal which exists in every human being, obscured for the most part by the necessities of the day, and in those even who hearken to its summons speaking so vaguely that all but one or two go out to 'follow wandering fires, lost in the quagmire.'"[5] Faintly or fervently they crave the sustenance and support of poetry, philosophy, religion. They rebel, however ineffectually, against an exclusive dedication to material interests and concerns. They find unsatisfying a routine of business and pleasure wherein, getting and spending, they lay waste their powers. In varying degrees of ardor they want to know more and learn more about the enjoyment of the arts and the utilization of spiritual values. Legitimately and inexorably they wish to deepen, broaden and enrich their lives.

[5] Paul Elmer More: *Shelburne Essays, Fourth Series,* "The Vicar of Morwenstow." © 1903-1934. Published by Houghton Mifflin Co.

A self-confessed neurotic pessimist, Mr. John Cowper Powys, in his *A Philosophy of Solitude* adumbrates much that constitutes the modern temper and the dilemma of the modern man. He finds life vapid and its savor bitter. He is profoundly unsatisfied with days dulled by moronic chatter, squirrel-in-treadmill professional activities, amusements which deplete rather than recreate and re-create bodily and mental health. In the twelfth century, as a disciple of Saint Bernard of Clairvaux, Mr. Powys might have found in an ordered existence of plain living, high thinking and the splendor of the liturgy some easement of his pain. But as a twentieth-century intellectual he can see in religious faith only a sentimental importance; to him the doctrines and practices which once were the most dynamic propulsive factors in human psychology are like a row of immemorial trees lining the road where toilers trudge to and fro—pleasing the eye, giving a little shade, at times making melancholy music. He believes in art; he does not believe in God. Tender and tolerant toward his discarded faith, even nostalgic and reverent, he feels within himself a lack, a void, a sense of restless unfulfillment.

Such men, and they are many, if too fastidious to lose themselves in drinking, dicing and drabbing, turn for assuagement to miscellaneous intellectual activity. So Mr. Powys sets forth his theory of Elementalism, an immersion in the phenomena and processes of nature. But nature, poor stepdame, cannot slake his drought. Nature worship, in one form or another tried over and over again, is never an adequate answer to spiritual cravings. Every man alive to in-

spiration gratefully knows that a measure of peace and renewal comes from a solitary walk in the pine woods, an hour
beside still waters, the contemplation of a hidden valley beneath the witchery of the moon. But only a measure. The
man-made world enslaves us, bruises us, wearies us, dissipates and depresses us, and earth and air and sea afford but
limited assuagement. Mr. Powys' Elementalism is a real but
pitifully partial palliative. Who drinks of the Brindisian foun-
tain shall thirst again; the breadfruit tree bears not the bread
of life.

Mr. Powys lucidly posits the problem of numerous men
and women of today. They have lost faith in religion; and
by a quirk of experience, unlooked for but inevitable, they
have lost likewise much of their once satisfying delight in
painting, poetry, music. If knowledge of the arts and fa-
miliarity with their master achievements automatically bestowed felicity, Mr. Powys would be the happiest man on
earth. A sub-surface unity inheres in spiritual experience.
The paths that lead to the spiritual summit differ in one
important respect from the paths that lead to the top of
Graylock or Pilatus; it is possible and desirable to ascend by
several of them simultaneously. He who deliberately refuses
to follow one of them may find his progress along another
path slackened or checked. This truth, so revealing and pene-
trating, Francis Thompson turned into glowing poetry in
"The Hound of Heaven."

The realm of spiritual values is a holy place, so it is fitting
that every man should rear within his soul a fane not made
with hands. It is a house of worship, a timeless shrine, a

dwelling place of peace. No pantheon designed for many gods, and no bleak meetinghouse severely unadorned, the Temple of the Spirit has walls indented with quiet chapels, a chancel ablaze with clustered votive lamps, and soaring windows of many-colored glass to filter the white radiance of eternity. Pendant bannerets and battle flags stained and tattered testify to struggles and triumphs in the unending strivings of man's highest aspirations against stupidity and greed and sloth. Stairways long and steep lead to the lofty spires,

> Whence men might see wide east and west in one
> And on one sea descend waned moon and mounting sun.

"Let us keep our silent santuaries," said Sénancour, "for within them are preserved the eternal perspectives."

The Temple of the Spirit is not erected by timid, arrogant or prosaic minds. The lower planes of intelligence, useful in logic-chopping, heresy hunting, computing one's income tax and circumventing one's neighbor in business are useless and even impedimental when the free soul undertakes the construction of his inner basilica. So are the flat head mistaking itself for the broad mind, the modern Dives in purple and fine linen, the callow scoffer at noble ideals and the trader who would taffic in them. The builder of the Temple of the Spirit has need to lift up mind and heart, to give glad and untrammeled response to the highest truth and brightest beauty he sees, to fling free of the suspicions and uncharities of sects and cliques and claques, to be open-minded yet dis-

23

criminating, gentle yet brave, ardent yet serene, eager and daring yet steadfast and enduring.

We see only that which we have it in us to see. Would we, as the Spanish proverb says, bring home the wealth of the Indies, we must fare forth with the wealth of the Indies. Writers and teachers intent on character building and the development of personality—despite their incidental abuse and degradation, both terms have vital significance—offer serviceable aids to the neophyte; but often they remind us of the optician who examines the ailing eye with scientific thoroughness but never thinks to inquire into the patient's general health and emotional habits and outlook on life. There is little advantage in expert advice on how to read a book, how to enjoy music or how to say a prayer unless it be conditioned by the pupil's existing knowledge, his likes and dislikes, his moral and spiritual case history, the extent to which he has drawn upon his cultural heritage. Habitually, when he gazes through the bars of this our mortal life, does he see mud or does he see stars?

Does he, to come to the heart of the matter, accept philosophy, religion and the arts as symbols of spiritual reality? Does he recognize that theology, metaphysics and literature are blueprints of a temple not made with hands? Does he concede that plan-reading is an art in itself and that the best blueprint ever devised may be misinterpreted by ignorant and untrained minds?

Against dullness, indifference, prejudice and pseudo-sophistication the gods strive in vain. Some men are too stubborn to enjoy music, too timid to follow the truth whithersoever it may lead, too absorbed in the lust of the flesh, the lust of the eyes—which is money-grubbing—and the pride of life to see and hear the angelic chorus on Bethlehem's holy night. The priceless vintage of the imponderables takes the shape of the human glasses into which it is poured. All of us were born ignorant, and in the realm of spiritual values many of us remain ignorant. Petty minds are accountable for pettiness in philosophy, religion and the arts. Only when we widen our horizons, discard our subservience to fads and vogues, and, in the words of Holy Writ, lift up our minds to heavenly desires, are we fit and ready to stand timeless and silent in the Temple of the Spirit.

II THE MEASURE OF A MAN

One tranquil evening two animate creatures gazed across a lake at the sun setting behind the serrated mountains. They were a lover and a cow. Motionless and intent, they looked much alike, and a naive psychologist might jump to the conclusion that they were similarly impressed by the sunset. But the cow, unable to discern the multicolored blazonry of clouds and shadowed canyons, stood in crass bovine beatitude, while the lover doubtless approximated to the lyric ecstasy of Jessica and Lorenzo in the moonlight at Belmont.

It would be untrue and unkind to say that two men contemplating the imponderables are as different as the lover and the cow contemplating the sunset; yet in reading Mr. Eliot's *The Waste Land* or Cicero's *De Senectute*, listening to a Stokowski-directed rendering of Prokofieff's *Overture Russe* or to the monks at Solesmes chanting the *Salve Regina*, watching Ethel Barrymore's revival of *A School for Scandal* or the last act of George Arliss' memorable production of *The Merchant of Venice*, Jones and Smith will experience divergent reactions. Why? Because, even as the lover and the cow are different animals, Jones and Smith are different men. They differ in intelligence and experience, in training

27

and cultural background, in mood and in temperament, which is habitual mood.

From Theophrastus down to Dr. William Sheldon, psychologists have sought to classify the varieties of human temperament. Long honored were the type divisions of "humors"—phlegmatic, choleric, melancholic and sanguine—formulated by Hippocrates. Devotees of astrology preferred a classification based on nativity stars; even those of us who regard astrology as a quaint and curious survival speak of temperaments as jovial, mercurial, saturnine. Yet another basis of classification is the resemblance of human beings to animals—the fox, the hog, the bull, the lion, the weasel. Jack London, who wrote three novels on the wolf theme, had a strikingly lupine grin. The harelip, the horseface, the elephantine tread are not, however, dependable indications of the habitual mood of their possessors—a truth made manifest by Rostand in *Cyrano de Bergerac* and by Mary Webb in *Precious Bane.* One of the most gentle and sensitive characters I have ever known was a man who looked and walked like a cross between the Emperor Caligula and a worn-out pugilist lamenting a wasted life.

In our day attempts to classify the temperaments are numerous, and, as might be expected, formidable with their words of learned length and thundering sound. Especially significant is Dr. Sheldon's division of the temperaments into the viscerotonic, the somatotonic and the cerebrotonic. More practical and popular is a fivefold classification: the vital, the motor, the osseous, the thoracic and the cerebral. Two points should be made clear at the outset of any consideration of

the temperaments: first, that a man's temperament is as un-
changeable as his bodily stature, the shape of his ears or his
skull capacity; secondly, that few if any men are entirely or
exclusively of any one temperament. But every man con-
forms predominantly with one of the five types.

The vital temperament is exemplified in the good, easy
man who enjoys food and drink and companionship, who
takes things as they come and is loath to lose sleep over either
a new heaven or a new earth: "What's the Constitution between friends?" It is averse from extremism and fanaticism,
cherishes creature comforts, favors domesticity, neighborli-
ness and tolerance. It makes a man a mixer, a joiner, a "regular guy," a bit sluggish in thought and a willing sharer of
sorrows and of joys. It is allergic to concentration, solitude
and silence. It responds to popular music, to pictures that
tell a story or enshrine a sentiment, to poetry that celebrates
home and mother, moonlight and honeysuckles, and recounts
deeds of derring-do. It favors a philosophy which buttresses
the virtues of family life and citizenship. Usually it clings
to the form of religion inculcated in youth, often retaining
childlike faith and childish superstitions; but it rarely runs to
excess of zeal and easily falls into neglect and indifference:
"I keep all the feasts, but I don't work hard at the fasts." In
general, the vital temperament stresses the livableness of
life: *Dum vivimus, vivamus.*

The man of motor temperament is the human machine. He
thrives on routine, regularity, the diurnal recurrence of a
familiar pattern of work and play, love and worship. A treadmill existence irks him not at all. He is ardently, often

blindly, loyal to a sect, a system, a way of life. He is the somatotonic truck horse as distinguished from the cerebrotonic race horse. He accepts responsibilities but dislikes to make decisions. Novelty of any kind repels and sometimes infuriates him. In philosophy and religion he will literally work at the theory of being and the salvation of his soul, and his working processes will be time-tested, conservative and largely rule-of-thumb. He welcomes detailed and methodical directions for detecting fallacies, teaching mathematics or examining his conscience. He wants a list of the world's best books, a summary of the great operas, an album of the most famous paintings; and he puts fervent faith in lectures and study courses on how to succeed in love and business. He is hostile to innovations in sculpture and architecture, though in controversies about the imponderables he prefers to wait and find out what the authorities have to say. He has no opinion of a new book until he has read a review of it or has heard somebody he respects discuss it. Like the little girl who had a little curl, when he is good he is very, very good, and when he is bad he is horrid. Of a motor-minded deacon of blameless life a vitalic critic said, "I could love that man if I were sure that just once in his life he was tempted to steal a calf or elope with Ninon de L'Enclos."

The man of osseous temperament is instinctively the boss. He loves to take charge, to give orders, to snipe at his superiors and to put his inferiors in their place. He resents even friendly and constructive criticism and is ruthless and vindictive in "purging" rivals and rebels. He is hard as nails, thick-skinned as a pachyderm. Seldom will he admit himself in the

30

wrong, for that, he fears, would lessen his prestige, weaken his authority. He would rather be president than be right. His participation in discussion, of the imponderables or of anything else, is assertive and argumentative and infused with missionary zeal; he wants to convert, not to contribute. He will eagerly organize and administer whatever comes to hand—deck games, a spelling bee, a sewing society, the finances of a municipality or the liturgy of a church. He thrives on the principle, Get out or get in line! Frequently he himself gets out; through the centuries rebels, dissenters, heresiarchs and reformers have invariably been osseous.

"Oh, for a life of sensations rather than of thoughts!" is the heart cry of the man of thoracic temperament. To him beauty is truth. He is imaginative, sensitive, mercurial, ardent but inconstant in love and work and play. No slave of habit, he resents routine; he is restless and ebullient, often shy and impractical. He illustrates the emotional instability accountable for the so-called artistic temperament—which sometimes is just plain temper. In the arts he is the creator and the appreciator as well. In philosophy he is never an Aristotelian or a Thomist, always a Platonist and an Augustinian. He vexes the motor mind and the cerebral mind through his passionate adherence to right ideas for wrong reasons. His fine frenzy infuriates the osseous mind, for the thoracic man either refuses to take orders or else executes them in a spirit the reverse of their issuance. He is unpredictable, adoring what he has burnt and burning what he has adored. In religion he is at once the childlike disciple and the problem child. In conduct he alternates prodigality with selfishness. Of Huysman's conversion to Catholicism a motor-minded cleric commented: "I am not wholly reassured. He did not fall into the arms of Mother Church according to the rules." The thoracic man never falls into anybody's arms according to the rules.

Rodin's "Le Penseur" is the cerebral temperament in stone. Indifferent to food and clothes, uncomfortable in a crowd, bored by conventionalities and driven mad by clichés and potted platitudes, the cerebral man might appositely exclaim, "Oh, for a life of thoughts rather than of sensations!" He is dissatisfied with the accepted explanations of man and the universe, contemptuous of popular standards of values. He questions, he doubts, and his skepticism may or may not lead to deeper insights. While the motor man accepts philosophy as a deposit of intellectual faith and the thoracic man as Plato's "child of wonder," to the cerebral man philosophy is an unusually persistent effort to think clearly. He wants to think, even if he doesn't know how to think. Often he is a radical, a crank, a nonconformist. Also he is a trail blazer, a discoverer, a pioneer. In religion the cerebral man, be he lay or clerical, believer or denier, is the perennial theologian; he demands reasons for the faith or the unfaith that is in him. The village atheist who taught his dog to howl every time the church bells started to ring was cerebral with a delicious touch of the thoracic. A picture or a drama, a poem or a piece of music gives the cerebral man a springboard for thinking out underlying and associated philosophies, historical germinations and sociological trends. He mixes his own highballs.

It would be pleasant and not unprofitable for the reader to

make a discreet survey of friends and acquaintances—and even relatives—in the light of the five temperaments; also to recall characters in history, including current history, and in the representative literature of the world. Was not Adam vital and Eve thoracic, he a bromide and she a sulphite? Julius Caesar was osseous, with a considerable touch of the vital; and osseous also were John Knox and John Calvin, Pope Boniface VIII and Oliver Cromwell, Catherine of Russia and Cardinal Manning. Among celebrities possessed of the motor temperament were the Emperor Augustus, Copernicus, Madame de Maintenon, President Madison, William Wordsworth, Phillips Brooks, Charles Stewart Parnell and Émile Zola. It would be easy to list instances of the thoracic temperament: think of Peter the Hermit, George Sand, John Barrymore. Of the vital type were Alcibiades, Cleopatra, Henry VIII and Erasmus, the latter with a strong infiltration of the cerebral. Predominantly cerebral were men otherwise dissimilar—Spinoza, Renan, Thomas Paine, Coleridge and John Stuart Mill.

Discussion of such lists may and possibly should lead to differences of judgment, but disputes will be tempered by remembering that a man's temperament is disclosed in the prevailing tenor of his life, not necessarily in isolated episodes. Thus Wordsworth and Parnell belong, or so it seems to me, in the motor category, notwithstanding that girl in France and Mrs. William O'Shea. Erasmus, as his letters abundantly prove, was mainly concerned with vital considerations—food and patronage and pocket money and convivial friendship—though he was immersed in intellectual interests and laid the egg that Luther hatched. Finally, before arguing for or against any inclusion, we must accept the fact that a man is neither damned nor beatified by being placed in any of the five categories. One temperament is not morally better or worse than another. There have been saints and sinners in all of them, and every temperament has contributed its quota of genius.

No man is under the sway of his temperament twenty-four hours a day. His habitual mood is now and then replaced by a mood which may mystify his friends and surprise himself. The vital man may occasionally decline a second drink, the motor man may develop a brief spurt of originality, the osseous man may once in a blue moon utter a sincere *mea culpa,* the thoracic man may briefly indulge in regimented living or transform himself into a thinking machine, the cerebral man may have spells of unreasoning emotion. Such assertion of an alien mood is especially marked in men of the thoracic and the cerebral temperament, for both detach themselves in some degree from normal living, and human nature thus denied will at times reassert itself and demand compensations. James Huneker showed insight when he wrote, "Scratch an artist and you surprise a child." There are times when the thoracic genius acts like a little boy, sometimes a rather naughty one. As for the thinker, when he falls in love he is likely to be a ravening wolf; instincts long ignored prove momentarily imperious. So it is that the thoracic man usually makes a splendid lover and a difficult husband, unlike the vital man, who is exactly the reverse—no young Lochinvar, but capable of being housebroken. Maybe poetic justice triumphs in the case of the osseous man who, having lost interest in one girl because she refused to quit tinting her fingernails and in another because she liked to read Verlaine, marries a demure-seeming Xantippe and degenerates into a connubial mouse.

Hamlet—with Hamlet left out—affords a fruitful field for a study of the temperaments. Vital are the King and Queen, Claudius enjoying noise and company, drinking and dancing; he "keeps wassail, and the swaggering up-spring reels." When in a difficulty he usually manages to win over an opponent like Laertes by putting an arm about his shoulders and giving him a man-to-man "selling talk." Hamlet's mother is equally vital in her lush affection for everybody, her complete lack of cerebral interests, her habit of taking refuge in sentimental clichés:

> Thou know'st 'tis common; all that lives must die,
> Passing through nature to eternity.

Gertrude and Claudius are obviously vital in their real if guilty affection and in their fondness for amorous dallying.

The boys from Wittenberg are one hundred per cent motor and as alike as the Gold Dust Twins. Rosencrantz and Guildenstern exemplify snobbery complacent and complete. They value the university atmosphere because it brings them into association with persons of importance and even eventuates in an invitation to the royal court of Denmark. Both are blood brothers to the brainless fraternity snobs who, thanks to "good contacts," become stamp-lickers or bond salesmen and follow the formal round of lodge chairs. At its best, the motor temperament is seen in Horatio, unshakably loyal, flawlessly tactful, pleasingly commonplace, unobtrusively helpful, faithful to confidences, happy to shine in the reflected light of a richer personality.

Laertes is thoracic; witness his impatience to be off for greener fields, his emotional advice to Ophelia, his berserk fury on his return from Paris, his melodramatic grief at his sister's funeral, his futile last-minute disclosure of the plot against Hamlet's life. His father, on the contrary, is an impressive exemplification of the osseous temperament. Polonius seethes and bubbles with plans and plots, schemes and explanations. He is impervious to suggestions. He is sure he knows everything and can arrange anything. He gives the high-strung Laertes a long-winded array of copybook maxims, pokes his paternal nose into Ophelia's intimacy with Hamlet, takes complete charge of things when the King seeks to spy on the Prince, and appropriately meets death while playing detective. Polonius was much more than a tedious old fool. Behind him he had a long and probably brilliant diplomatic career; but, like so many other osseous worthies, he had missed too many boats, had failed to recognize the time to retire. His was not the wisdom of the Latin-American dictator who said: "A ruler should know in the seat of his pants when he ought to get out of his chair."

Conceivably the world would be a better place if every man were in the profession or occupation most in harmony with his native temperament. As things are, and despite the often commendable acumen of personnel experts, we have teachers who are anything but vital, bookkeepers who are poets frustrate, philosophers so completely motor that they think philosophy is book learning, and administrators with no tincture of the osseous in their souls. The down-to-earth Clown, the broad comedy First Grave-Digger is the most distinctively cerebral character in *Hamlet*. He is a rabid individualist. He loves to argue, often sophistically, and to disagree tartly with the fools and the knaves he finds his fellow men to be. He is touchily class-conscious: "The more pity that great folk should have countenance in this world to drown or hang themselves, more than their even-Christian." He can dilate on how long a man lies in the earth ere he rot —"A tanner will last you nine year"—but he is impersonal and objective in his attitude to the fact of death; skulls and bones are strictly scientific items. Unabashed by gentility or education, he delights to make the urbane and thoughtful Prince of Denmark a target for his sallies—more so indeed than he makes his moronic assistant. Incidentally, like a good many other cerebral people, he does surprisingly little work; I have never seen a production of *Hamlet* without wondering how Ophelia's grave came to be readied at all.

Each man's approach to the Temple of the Spirit is manifestly modified by that man's temperament. You take the high road and I'll take the low road. Johann Strauss the elder was of the motor temperament, and his sense of musical values differed widely from his son's. The younger Strauss was mainly thoracic, and both in composing and conducting flouted many of the procedures inculcated by his father. Yet both the Strausses brought important contributions to the Vienna they knew. Each learned a discipline and evolved a technique; the discipline and technique of the son would have been utterly unsuitable for the father. When artists quarrel and thinkers wrangle and holy men bark and bite, it is mainly due to what in the euphemism of the divorce courts is called incompatibility of temperament. In the Temple of the Spirit there are enough chapels to gratify the needs and preferences of all who enter. For each and for all but one thing is necessary: Every worshiper must discipline himself.

The discipline imposed by the school principal, the top sergeant, the traffic officer is an external discipline which ordinarily cannot modify and adapt its rulings to suit individual requirements. That is why in so many instances it fails to produce any profound and permanent improvement. Obviously, external discipline is better than no discipline at all, and to men of some temperaments, as we have already implied, it is the only sort of discipline that is acceptable. Other men, though never embarrassingly numerous, outgrow certain phases of external discipline, no longer needing some of its imposed aids; when a man is self-disciplined in his relations with the imponderables he is, rightly, less dependent on extraneous directives and controls than are the novice and the neophyte. Some forms of external discipline are like a knowledge of grammar—a good thing to get and then to forget. The self-disciplined man can pursue his ideals in harmony with the needs of his temperament—including the need of curbing the extravagances into which it might lead him. He will not permit a system of discipline, however salutary, to harden into a mechanical routine or exalt it into an end in itself. An elaborate scaffolding may be necessary in the construction of the Temple of the Spirit, but the scaffolding is a temporary device and no part of the finished building.

For men of all temperaments mere vague benevolence and wishful thinking will not automatically generate "the breadth of vision, the independence of judgment, the tolerance and magnanimity" [1] which are the fruits of participation in spiritual values. A shrewd librarian once remarked: "There is one kind of reader who just tickles a book and then expects to look like the man in the advertisement for the Harvard Classics." To tickle a book, to toy with religion, to flirt with philosophy and the arts is to desecrate the imponderables. Not thus will spiritual truth rejuvenate the individual and the world. Truth, beauty and goodness are not ideals to be honored merely, but to be lived; they are not period pieces to be displayed in a showroom, but energizing forces to be inducted into our spiritual blood stream.

The human race, for all its follies and frailties, has learned something during the few centuries of our civilization. More accurately, wise and observant individuals in every age have garnered the fruits of wisdom and preserved them in such vital volumes as the odes of Horace, the letters of Cicero, the essays of Bacon, Goethe, Emerson, Evelyn Underhill and Bishop John Lancaster Spalding. Differing as inspirational writers do in temperament, in outlook, in cultural background, they nevertheless agree in stressing the necessity for a man to prove himself, to make himself over, when he ap-

[1] W. Somerset Maugham: *Introduction to Modern English and American Literature.*

proaches the Temple of the Spirit. Call it what you will—and to men of certain temperaments nomenclature is very important—some sort of discipline is indispensable. Knowledge —not necessarily scholarship—is one element thereof, knowledge paid for in hours of systematic study. Another element of basic discipline is the control and regulation of natural tendencies and appetites, for pride and lust and gluttony cloud the soul and dull the mind and weaken the aspirations after spiritual reality which most men, however faintly, entertain. Even the most convivial of the sages recommend periods of withdrawal from the ways and works of the world, to grow in solitude and silence and secure a steady and balanced perspective. And they urge the need of faith and love, of meditation and guidance, of independence and the spirit of reverence. Some of their counsels are consonant with the time-spirit of our day and win easy acceptance; other counsels run counter to current fashions in thought and are perhaps repulsive to our personal temperament. But all their counsels are sage and salutary. "Pure gold," says a Chinese proverb, "does not fear the furnace."

Not all the details of that cumulative wisdom are of equal value, however, and one item of it Jones may urgently require and Smith may casually neglect, for Jones, let us say, is mainly motor and Smith mainly thoracic; so Jones needs to cultivate independence and avoid fossilized routine, while Smith needs to bridle his extravagant impulses and make his mind keep office hours. The cerebral man is prone to assume that every man is his own pope, the thoracic man to accept his fluctuating feelings as a dependable guide, the osseous man to impose upon himself and others the efficiency-expert attitude, the vital man to suspect anything that interferes with his comfort and convenience, the motor man to enslave himself to methods and formulas and maxims. Motor, surely, was the hypochondriac who cabled from San Francisco to Paris to find out if his physician permitted him to have a baked apple at breakfast.

The man of the vital, the motor or the osseous temperament is the extrovert; he is centrifugal in his life pattern, for his center is largely outside himself. He depends on other people, on institutions, on arbitrary standards and social conventions, even when, as sometimes happens, his attitude toward them is inimical; though it is hell to be with them, it is more acutely hell to be without them. His general direction is *into* life. The introvert, on the contrary, is centripetal; thoracic or cerebral, he revolves on his own ectomorphic axis. His general direction is *away from* life. Let the heavens fade and the hills dissolve, let empires decay and the great globe itself leave not a rack behind, the introvert continues to inhabit a world of his own. Applause and approbation, without which the extrovert cannot live, affect the introvert hardly at all; though he is abnormally sensitive and suffers keenly, he recalls Chesterton's description of Cardinal Newman, "a naked man who carried a naked sword." The imbalances existing in the two types are less marked when there is a blending of vital and thoracic, motor and cerebral; but even then inner conflicts and outer inconsistencies will arise. What a piece of work is man!

Our hope, and by no means a forlorn hope, is in the world

of the imponderables. We shall not radically alter the temperament which is ours, but in the realm of spirit we shall at least find incentives and aids to internal poise and external equilibrium. No miracle-working shrine, the Temple of the Spirit will not reshape our errant noses, restore graying hair or fallen arches, or endow us—in heaven's name, why should it?—with perpetual youth. But within its cool and reassuring walls we shall find self-knowledge and self-discipline. We shall learn to utilize even the defects of our virtues and the limitations of our qualities. And happiness in some degree may come to us unsought as we gaze out on the world and the ways of men through

> Charm'd magic casements, opening on the foam
> Of perilous seas . . .

III HOLY GROUND

MOSES, the great Hebrew leader, had a long and varied preparation for his exalted mission. Danger he knew and privation, and the salt savor of the bread of others. He learned the lessons of life through a spell of luxury at the court of Egypt and through years of seclusion in Midian, a stranger in a strange land. He knew likewise the disordered impulses of his own errant heart—sudden fears and rising rages and now and again a paralyzing sense of his own deficiencies. But when he heard the voice of the Lord from the midst of the burning bush he was to learn the most fundamental lesson of all: "Put off thy shoes from off thy feet, for the place whereon thou standest is holy ground." It was needful that the man whose spiritual contributions, to his own people and to Western civilization, should develop within himself a reverence for things sacred and sublime.

Flippancy, censoriousness and vulgarity go far to explain why many men fail to recognize and esteem the imponderables; but the chief obstacle, decisive as blindness and implacable as death, is lack of the spirit of reverence. To get we must give, and what we give is homage—in art and thought, in life and literature. The Philistine in the arts, the denier in religion, are both marked by an underdevelopment

of what the jargon of phrenology called the bump of veneration. If we lack the spirit of reverence our eyes are held
from the beauty of a landscape or a painting, and the well-
wrought and revealing passages in Aeschylus or Dante or
Shakespeare will seem but a string of conceits, a resonant
rhapsody of words. Reverence signs with its impassioned
seal the lunatic, the lover and the poet. Yes, the lunatic, for
from the point of view of unsympathetic common sense any
manifestation of reverence seems a little mad. To the cynic
and the misanthrope the lover is silly, and to the man who
has no music in his soul the poet is a weaver of demented
dreams.

Mr. Worldly Wiseman experiences no glow of reverence at
sight of the pilgrim and the saint. He reserves his admiration
and adoration for the exponent of material values. To religion he may give lip service, but the spectacle of somebody
actually practicing its precepts and shaping his daily life in
consonance with spiritual principles makes him distinctly uncomfortable and sometimes unaccountably indignant. Don't
be an ass! It simply isn't done, if you know what I mean!
Those hard sayings of Christ—sell all, love your enemies,
turn the other cheek, seek first the Kingdom—are all very
well in their way, but they must be interpreted with discretion and without prejudice to Mr. Worldly Wiseman's bodily
comfort and social status and rating in Bradstreet. He regards men like Saint Francis of Assisi and Savonarola, John
Wesley and General Booth as perverse and unbalanced. And
he harbors an undiscriminating disapproval of the priest in
politics. Reverence for things spiritual? That is inconceivable

as selfless love for a polyhedron or an ecstatic delight in wood ticks. My shoes from off my feet, indeed! Yes, if I can sell the shoes at a profit. Otherwise, no bare feet in the presence of a dozen burning bushes!

After many a summer dies the swan, and Mr. Worldly Wiseman would rather not think about it; he is allergic to Cicero's noble conviction that death is "the summons and release of God." Rome's least mortal mind wins no response from Mr. Worldly Wiseman, to whom *mors janua vitae* is in two senses an alien utterance; he sees death not as the gateway to life but the trap door to nothingness. And his phobia is contagious, even fashionable. In fact, our reluctance to use the words death and dead at all, while otherwise priding ourselves on calling a spade a spade, is symptomatic of a general failure to follow the imponderables as pillars of cloud and of fire. One might discover ample evidence to sustain the thesis that the only men who face death bravely, calmly and in some instances gladly, are artists and thinkers, poets and saints.

> I fancy it isn't the men who get most out of the world and are always buoyant and cheerful that most fear to die. Rather it is the weak-engined souls, who go about with dull eyes, that cling most fiercely to life. They have not the joy of being alive which is a kind of earnest of immortality.[1]

Reverence for spiritual values comes not from weak-engined souls. The life they so desperately cling to is the life of Mr.

[1] John Buchan: *Greenmantle,* p. 435. © 1916, 1944. Published by Houghton Mifflin Co.

Worldly Wiseman; and to the light of eternity, reflected in music and painting, philosophy and religion, their dull eyes are pathetically blind.

In any comprehensive conception of education as a process of complete living and a preparation therefor, it should be axiomatic that a primary function of the teaching process is a vital inoculation of the virtue of reverence, a sane and steadfast development of the pupil's bump of veneration. In the supreme epochs of educational history—in fifth-century Athens, in the flowering of Scholasticism, in the ripeness of the Renaissance and here and there in our own country and our own time—this has indeed been an honored objective. The very extravagances into which some noble educational enterprises have slipped—the worship of Aristotle, a narrow and narrowing absorption in an exclusive aestheticism and the dismissal of certain fields of human knowledge as unworthy and unscholarly—are but incidental defects, however deplorable, in the exercise of a living, leaping zeal for this or that spiritual value. If theologians have been traditionally bad-tempered, it is due less to celibacy or malnutrition than to reverent devotion to a dogma or a master, passionate loyalty to a way of thinking or a school of thought. And if influential painters and musicians are frequently intolerant, it is chiefly because of their ardent dedication to the Pre-Raphaelites or Picasso, Brahms or Berlioz. Teachers of history like Mommsen and Lord Acton, John Fiske and Henry Morse Stephens unconsciously stimulated bumptious irritability in their more suggestible pupils, for the disciple is not always greater than the master. But in all such instances the root of the offending was reverent absorption in scholarly ideals impugned and insulted by scoffers and cynics. The students had heard a voice from out the burning bush. Occasionally they were a little too hasty in smiting rocks; but at least they had put off their shoes from off their feet.

In our schools and universities there would seem to be no embarrassing plethora of burning bushes and the generality of students are suspiciously well shod. The bump of veneration is as completely discredited as the pseudo-science which once capitalized upon it. From kindergarten up to graduate school sundry virtues are inculcated, but reverence for the imponderables is not one of them. Shortsightedly our educators have overemphasized material interests and concerns. They have dignified the legitimate training of the body with the anomalous name of physical education, forgetting that apart from the imponderables the word education has no meaning whatever.

Some years ago a university president was conducting a group of visitors over his extensive campus. A new gymnasium was nearing completion, and he pointed out the elaborate rose window in the south wall. One of his guests, who had caught the spirit of Mont-Saint-Michel and Chartres— from both Henry Adams' book and the historic churches themselves—expressed surprise at the incongruous inclusion of distinctively religious art in a building designed for basket ball and calisthenics. Whereupon the president boomed: "That, my dear sir, exemplifies the modern conception of education. We are frankly complacent over this triumph of functional architecture. That window is not a decorative detail; it is a sacred symbol. We feel that stained glass, formerly associated with houses of worship, has its logical place in a gymnasium. For we believe profoundly in the religion of the body, and that rose window will inspire both students and instructors to esteem physical education as something high and holy."

In the name of education we have evolved courses in business English and commercial Spanish, ignoring the fact that good English is, as Swift long ago pointed out, proper words in proper places, and that the distinctive glory of the Hispanic tongue has had but slight dependence on commercial relations. In philosophy we have blighted the spirit of reverence by subjecting every school of thought to an analytical scrutiny boastfully impartial—and as egregiously infertile as a spavined mule. We have "enriched" the curriculum by suffocating its soul. "Our pedagogical high priests," writes Dr. E. W. Knight in *Progress and Educational Perspective*,* "say that the important thing in education is not ideas or knowledge but attitudes and the thinking process. But how good attitudes and sound thinking can be developed without good ideas, sound knowledge and accurate information, the pedagogical Brahmans never take time to explain."

In the teaching of even so spiritual a subject as literature the eternal perspectives are befogged, and admiration for depth of thought, felicity of expression and sweep and splendor of inspiration is virtually nonexistent. The very adjective literary makes many scholars jeer or see red. Cicero's worshipful memories of Cato, Dante's respect and affection for

* ©1942 by Kappa Delta Pi. Published by The Macmillan Co.

Virgil, Ben Jonson's regard "this side idolatry" for Shake-speare stimulate but slight imitation in high-school classes and university seminars. Plenty of professors have gone to Greece, but the late William Lyon Phelps was the only one to tell us that on landing at Patras—least attractive of Pelo-ponnesian cities—he fell upon his knees and kissed the sacred soil. The poet-professor, Father John B. Tabb, after reading to his class a passage from Milton or Browning, would blink behind his thick glasses and exclaim: "My, my, if I could only write like that!" Even the dullest pupil caught something of his glowing reverence. I fear the perennial sophomore would curl a contemptuous lip at such enthusiasm, for to him literature is something to be picked at, dissected, traced to its alleged sources and superciliously criticized in the flickering light of current political and economic theories, not something to be admired, reveled in and inspired by, something fair and precious to be devoutly wrought into the structure of the Temple of the Spirit.

Among pedagogical practices deservedly held in honor, dis-cussion performs a useful, an indispensable function. Educa-tion is not a one-way street but a vital contact of mind with mind; the mind of the pupil is not a barrel to be filled but a riv-ulet to be guided to limitless seas. Yet, as it is carried on in nu-merous classrooms, discussion degenerates into brash and con-temptuous comment, the belittling of high ideals and master spirits. Its objective is to get the student to express himself, even when he has nothing of value to express. It obscures and shrivels rather than expands and enlightens the mind. It fosters the pernicious error that one man's opinion is as true

and trustworthy as any other man's, that the stripling fresh-
man with no intellectual background and little insight into
the variant bypaths of the human heart, is culturally on a
par, not only with his instructor—a supposition at least de-
batable—but with Plato and Spinoza, Horace and Tennyson,
Pico della Mirandola and Maurice Barrès. It breeds cocksureness, arrogance and conceit; it fails to foster reverence
for the best that has been known and thought.

At its worst and at its best the art of discussion was keenly
evaluated by William Hazlitt:

> In general, wit shines only by reflection. You must take your
> cue from your company—must rise as they rise and sink as they
> fall. You must see that your good things, your knowing allu-
> sions, are not flung away, like the pearls in the adage. What a
> check it is to be asked a foolish question; to find that the first
> principles are not understood! You are thrown on your back
> immediately; the conversation is stopped like a country-dance
> by those who do not know the figure. But when a set of adepts,
> of *illuminati,* get about a question, it is worth while to hear
> them talk. They may snarl and quarrel over it, like dogs; but
> they pick it bare to the bone—they masticate it thoroughly.[2]

The Boy Jesus in the midst of the Temple doctors exemplified discussion at its best: He was found "hearing them and
asking them questions." And the fruitage of that discussion
was reverance: His hearers were astonished at His wisdom
and His answers. Astonishment is occasionally aroused by
the *illuminati* contributing to discussions in college classes
and the after-lecture period of community forums, but rarely

[2] "On the Conversation of Authors."

does it induce anything remotely resembling reverence for
first principles or any principles. Seldom do thoughts
"bubble up and sparkle like beads on old wine," seldom does
discussion leave a flavor "like fine green tea"; rather, it leaves
the bad taste of Hazlitt's "self-taught man, with the repulsive
self-sufficiency which arises from an ignorance of what hun-
dreds of men have known before him." "In pronouncing
judgment," says Quintilian, "we should be modest and circumspect, lest we condemn what we do not understand—a
thing which often happens."

Places there are, of course, where discussion is productive
of admiration for the imponderables. Those two splendid
teachers, Copeland of Harvard and Phelps of Yale, kindled a
reverential spirit in their students; so did the Columbia group
led by Mr. John Erskine and Mr. Herbert Hawkes; so do the
leaders of discussion at Saint John's College and men like
President Hutchins and Mr. Mortimer Adler at the University
of Chicago. From the interchange of ideas and impressions
and the art of thinking actively exercised, students—and
instructors too—derive incalculable benefit because they
bring to the discussion something they hold in common,
namely, a conviction of the continuity of our cultural tradition, an open-minded respect for vital books and disciplined
minds, fertile ideas and exalted ideals.

Anthropologists wisely warn us against assuming radical
differences between the races of mankind, and history makes
it fairly plain that Jew and Gentile, Finn and Frenchman
are brothers under the skin. Yet certain emotional habits and
social conventions differ in various nations and affect the

quality and degree of the citizen's reverence for the imponderables. Chesterton, a friendly observer of the Celt, once
wrote that every Irishman he met was secretly laughing at
every other Irishman—another way of saying that in Dublin
and Donegal you have to be very good at your art or very
genuine in your convictions if you hope to bring people to
their knees. In England that widely publicized racial reserve
often operates in the domain of the imponderables; the
Englishman can enjoy music and poetry as much as anybody
else but he shies away from manifesting excitement over them,
and he is embarrassed and repelled by extravagance in philosophy and extremism in religion. It is the Latins, including
the reputedly logical and sophisticated French, who respond
most readily to nonmaterial values. Observe, for instance,
how in the Romance languages the adjective *divine* is applied
to a poem, an actress, a school of thought. The teeming worship of their disciples followed Petrarca and Victor Hugo
everywhere, discomfiting the one and gratifying the other;
it was at times excessive and undiscriminating, but at least
it disclosed in its proponents a capacity for recognizing and
reverencing the things of the spirit. So did the *vivas* which
resounded from the gallery of the Metropolitan when Caruso
or Melba concluded an aria.

We in the United States, the offspring of all the peoples of
Europe, are prone to follow alternating ancestral trends. We
can be uproariously enthusiastic for a space, then as stolid as
a refrigerated fish. We ripe and ripe, and rot and rot. We
worship briefly and blindly; and presently we smash the god's
statue. Few are the cinema celebrities who enjoy a lengthy

tenure of popularity; were a blackout imposed on Hollywood
you could stroll by night down Vine Street in the light of
fallen stars. It is much the same with our most popular
writers; they have their day and cease to be. In music we dote
on Wagner, rave over Rachmaninoff, swing to "swing" and
away from it to "sweet." We are not wholly unlike the Athe-
nians whom Saint Paul reproved for being too superstitious;
we are intent ever on the very latest thing. Our reverence is
as fleeting as Herrick's roses; it is not the love that endures
and is patient.

Yet devotion to the imponderables, when sane and magnanimous and worthy of its objects, should burgeon and grow
as we widen our sympathies, deepen our insights and enrich
our lives. Timeliness, the quality of being up-to-date, has
nothing essential to do with religion or painting, music or
philosophy. It has nothing to do with acting either; in every
epoch of stage history there are simply good actors and bad
actors. Obsession with current events is a form of spiritual
suicide. Imposing its short-sighted restrictions, it hinders us
from seeing through the facts and conditions we are directly
looking at. Few of the club women and politicians intent on
improving our good-neighbor policy in the Western Hemi-
sphere perceive that the chief difference between Latin
Americans and us is that the Latin Americans still hold in
reverence the arts and traditional religion. Technological
courses, however necessary, and a journalistic interest in
world affairs, however alluring, alienate us from the humanis-
tic studies which inculcate respect for great art and reverence
for the finest and highest achievements of the human spirit.

When the world is too much with us we lose the eternal perspectives, we desert our silent sanctuaries, we concentrate on shifting expediency rather than on the abiding wisdom of the ages. It is impossible to be reverent toward the strident issues of the hour; and without reverence the people perish.

Dr. Dietrick von Hildebrand goes to the root of the matter:

> The lack of reverence may have two roots, and accordingly there are two different types of men wanting in reverence: The arrogant person and the senseless, blunt one. . . . The man who lacks reverence because of pride and arrogance approaches everything with conceit and presumption, imagines that he knows everything, that he sees through everything. . . . He thinks himself always greater than that which is not himself.
>
> The concupiscent man is interested in the world only as a means in procuring him pleasure. . . . He does not face the world with arrogance and conceit, but with a blunt stupidity. Stubbornly imprisoned in his own self, he violates being, and seeing it only from the outside, he thus misses its true meaning.[3]

Taken in the right sense, the saying is true that man is the measure of all things. But the right sense accepts man at his highest and best, and certainly does not hold that *man* is equivalent to *a man*. Joe Doakes or Mrs. Malaprop is not the measure of all things. We have schools and colleges where Joe Doakes and Mrs. Malaprop may learn that there have been wiser and keener and nobler men and women than they, that in the imponderables are embodied the standards of

---

[3] *Liturgy and Personality*, pp. 59-60. © 1943 by the author. Published by Longmans, Green & Co.

values which man uses to measure all things. From the proud and the sensual that knowledge is withheld.

Shallow minds are incapable of reverence, for reverence implies generosity, magnanimity, greatness of soul. The big mind responds to the note of wonder and the challenge of adventure in the deeper reaches of existence. It delights to give allegiance to something bigger, finer, nobler than itself. The little mind, often cunning and clever, measures the universe with a homemade yardstick, digs a hole in the sand and tries to pour the ocean into it; the big mind, convinced of its own littleness, accepts the measuring rod of the infinite; it revels in the splendor of the deep-voiced sea and accepts on faith the expanses of ocean lying beyond the horizon of its vision and experience. Without the spirit of reverence there can be no creative action in art, religion, philosophy; and without it there can be no vital appreciation of the imponderables.

The reverent mind does not strain after the startling and sensational; it is indifferent to a so-called originality motivated by what Saintsbury dismissed as "the vulgar fear of the commonplace and obvious." While shunning sentimentality, it cleaves to sentiment—a distinction which Goethe drew in reaching his estimate of *I Promessi Sposi;*

> Manzoni's inner culture here appears so high that scarcely anything can approach it. It satisfies us like perfectly ripe fruit. . . . His feeling for every situation is manly and genuine.[4]

[4] *Conversations with Eckermann,* July 18, 1827.

Reverence is not incompatible with a lively recognition of the incongruous and the absurd. Humor is no road block on the path to the imponderables. Most of the world's supreme writers were humorists in season. The gargoyles of Rheims and Notre Dame, the wood carvings in Swiss and German churches, are proof that in the ages of faith cathedral building was a serious but not a lugubrious business. Plenty of saints could laugh as abdominally as Rabelais. As for philosophers, they could do with a Democritus or two, for their conspicuous shortcoming is to take themselves with pompous solemnity. The Three Tailors of Tooley Street—"We, the people of England"—didn't think themselves funny, either. What shrivels the capacity to appreciate the higher life values is not humor, but the effort to achieve it by men on whose nativity a star declined to dance.

Nor does reverence imply blindness to the imperfections and perversities of persons dedicated to spiritual interests and of institutions through which we maintain relations with the imponderables. It is stupid to denigrate Poe's poetry because, reputedly, Poe couldn't carry his liquor, to repudiate the *philosophia perennis* because some phases of it may seem needlessly abstruse, to turn away from the religious interpretation of man and the universe on account of lazy monks and lustful parsons, clerical covetousness and sectarian strife. Realistic in outlook and blessed with a sense of proportion, the magnanimous man is neither shocked nor alienated by the lack of perfection in a palpably imperfect world. The very existence of counterfeit coin proves that there must be lawful money. The canker in the rose need not detract from

56

our enjoyment of the rose; poets have discerned in blight but an enhancement of beauty. Reverent if unconventional was the man who remarked, apropos of laxness and venality in Rome, "You shouldn't be astonished to find a little manure at the root of the tree."

More than twenty years ago, on the Day of All Souls, I visited the Cemetery of Père-Lachaise in Paris. The sky was overcast, the air was chill, and upon the gravel paths lay the wetness of the preceding night's showers. Before the tomb of Chopin two well-dressed young men knelt in the mud and offered silent prayers. They had brought waxen tapers which they placed upon the stone, and with their hands they sheltered the reluctant flames. Oblivious of passers-by, the young Parisians kept their devout vigil beneath Clésinger's sculptured portrait of the Polish master. Their names, their status, their subsequent careers are of course unknown to me; it is enough to know that within their souls glowed a profound reverence for the imponderables.

Something of their devotion is necessary for all of us who would live serenely and fruitfully in the Temple of the Spirit. In the presence of spiritual values we are wise to light our candles and guard the sacred flame. To the young men kneeling in the irrelevant mud of Père-Lachaise, Chopin's soaring tender tonalities, colorful and alluring as a tropical sunset, had opened a vista into the world of abiding beauty. More than seventy years had passed since the October day when the Polish pianist was borne from the Madeleine to the solemn rhythm of his own B flat minor Funeral March, but to the watchers at his grave his gay mind and sad heart still spoke in his flaming Polonaises, his melancholy Mazurkas and the waltz he had composed in the rain-pelted monastery of Valdemosa, spoke with

. . . prophetic
Lips hot with the blood-beats of song.

IV THE CLEAN OF HEART

WHEN we use the word *law*, as when we say, "There ought to be a law prohibiting gum-chewing," or "You are violating a basic law of life," it is seemly to be aware of the species of law we have in mind. Is it a law enacted by legitimate authority, such as the municipal ordinance which forbids smoking on streetcars, or the law promulgated by certain church organizations which forbids a minister to smoke anywhere? Is it a law proceeding from usage, which frowns on the locution, "I don't know nothing nohow," or condemns our saying *cary* when we mean *carry*, and Uncle Hairy when we mean Uncle Harry? Is it a law founded on precedent, such as the law which supports the right of eminent domain? Is it a law based on the observation of phenomena, such as the law of gravitation? It is in this last sense that the word is used when we speak of the laws of nature, the laws of being, the laws of the spiritual world.

The laws of the spiritual world in some respects parallel the laws of the material world and in other respects run contrary to them. Truth is to the mind as food is to the body, for instance, and the processes of intellectual digestion and metabolism resemble the corresponding physiological processes. But when Christ declared, "He that would save his life

59

must lose it," He formulated a spiritual law that has no counterpart in the material order. In the fields of both matter and spirit men do not gather grapes of thorns or figs of thistles. On the other hand, as Tennyson tunefully explains in the "Bugle Song" from *The Princess*, the physical laws of sound have no validity in the spiritual world; the echoes of the bugle gradually die away, while the echoes of human personality often wax increasingly pervasive with the passing of time:

> Our echoes roll from soul to soul,
> And grow for ever and for ever.

"As a child," writes Mr. Julian Green, "I used to wonder how it was that, being gifted with the power to see in all directions in the physical world, we could see only back of us and never ahead when it came to looking into time." [1] Wonder, a salutary emotion, was induced through the perception of a difference between material and spiritual laws.

The spiritual laws that correspond with the laws of the natural world and the spiritual laws that bear no resemblance to physical laws are equally real and valid. Failure to see that some spiritual laws resemble natural laws and others do not accounts for the error of looking upon everything natural as evil and accursed, as well as the opposite error of assuming that the summation of human wisdom is to follow nature. In the realm of the imponderables we have at

---

[1] *Memories of Happy Days*, p. 130. © 1942. Published by Harper & Brothers.

times to do violence to nature. On that point all vital religions agree; and frequently the arts, in their manifestations, ignore and transcend nature. Beethoven baffles the listener who expects to find in music a literal reproduction of the physical world. Goya infuriates the observer who looks for meticulous fidelity to human anatomy. Browning's Andrea del Sarto falls short of artistic greatness precisely because he is "the fault-less painter." On the stage we learn to accept distortions of real life. Every room has a fourth wall which is no wall at all, and it is correct but irrelevant to say that no military leader ever made the kind of speech Shakespeare's King Henry V delivers at Harfleur. All the arts avail themselves of poetic license. The imponderables, each in its own way, may and sometimes must rise above the laws of the natural world.

One spiritual law of scope and importance is luminously expounded by Dante,[2] the far-reaching truth that in the realm of the imponderables the material element of quantity has no place. In the physical order, obviously, quantity means much, and sometimes everything. If I have a loaf of bread and give half of it away, I have only half a loaf left. If I have ten dollars and give five dollars away, I have only five dollars left. If I have three acres of land and give one acre away, I have only two acres left. And this law of quan-tity is not affected by my motives in the transaction. I may give away the bread because I can't eat it, and the money be-cause I wish to help a needy friend, and the land because I

[2] *Purgatorio*, xiv, 86-7, and xv, 45-75.

am tired of digging out stumps and clearing off weeds; but in each case, because I give, I have less.

The quantitative element, however, has no place in the world of the imponderables. There I can give, and yet sustain no deprivation,

> . . . since good, the more
> Communicated, more abundant grows.[3]

Abélard, instructing the ardent disciples who followed him out into the forest, lost none of his knowledge or his skill by sharing his ideas; if anything, he was, like all good teachers, enlarged and liberated by the act of teaching. When Mr. Olin Downes communicates to New York readers his impressions of the music festival at Stockbridge, he suffers no diminution of either enjoyment or scholarship. The Athenian throng that heard Demosthenes fulminate against Philip of Macedon went away with a heightened sense of patriotism, but they left the orator in no sense impoverished. Probably Kipling enjoyed himself when he wrote "Mandalay" and "The Cat That Walked by Himself"; his enjoyment was augmented rather than diminished by the enjoyment experienced by his readers. In the world of the imponderables the material law of conservation has no place:

[3] *Paradise Lost*, V, 71-2. The keen Miltonian may recall that the words are spoken by the Tempter in Eve's troubled dream; yet they are wise words and true. Satan, who assumes the appearance of an angel of light, speaks in the guise of a cosmic philosopher. To discount a wise utterance because of its source is to merit the reproach Iago hurls at Desdemona's father: "Zounds, sir, you are one of those who will not serve God, if the devil bid you."

True love in this differs from gold and clay,
That to divide is not to take away.[4]

In business, politics and social striving what one man gains
another man lacks; in the Temple of the Spirit what one man
wins another man wins too—"so much the more of good doth
each possess."

"O human race," cries Dante's Guido del Duca, "why dost
thou set thy heart there where exclusion of a companion is
necessary?" Why, that is, focus concern on material goods
and interests, the pursuit of which precludes the sharing of
them with others. Absorption in material things generates
the oppressor's wrong, the proud man's contumely, the in-
solence of office; it replaces inspiring emulation with cutthroat competition; it makes the love of money the root of
all evil. Lay not up treasures on earth, said the Master, but
treasures in heaven—otherwise, in Dante's words, "Because
you set your mind only on earthly things, you draw but darkness from the very light."

In *The New Western Front*, Mr. Stuart Chase points out
that wars are mainly the outcome of national absorption in
the goods which cannot be shared without diminution, that
imperialism, the systematic exploitation of small countries
to secure such goods, is the baleful cause of fratricidal and
suicidal strife. Profound and practical is his belief that universal brotherhood will cease to be a dream only when the
peoples of the earth learn to share with one another, not

---

[4] Shelley, *Epipsychidion*, 160-1.

their beef and oil, their grain and magnesium, but their music, their art, their literature, their constructive scholarship and their religious ideals. He lists items which should and should not be shared, and his classification of goods is based on the distinction between spiritual and material values. Despite the world-shaking developments that have taken place since it was written, his book is no more outmoded than the faith in spiritual values voiced by Juliet:

> My bounty is as boundless as the sea,
> My love as deep; the more I give to thee,
> The more I have, for both are infinite.

Inherent in those words is the distinction between love and lust, the one a spiritual experience, the other an animal urge. Juliet speaks a language incomprehensible to Casanova or Don Juan, the language of the clean of heart.

The clean of heart have been called blessed. But who are the clean of heart? Surely those men and women who cleave to spiritual values, for as Virgil explains to the still earthbound Dante, "The more the people who set their hearts on high, the more there are for loving well and the more love there is, and like a mirror one reflects to the other." The clean of heart, through religion pure and undefiled, find union with things eternal. The clean of heart, through immersion in philosophic thought, learn with Boethius to fling free of the trammels of circumstance and the slavery of worldly ambitions. The clean of heart rise on the wings of music and poetry until, with Dante in the *Paradiso*, they may look down on the frenzied and futile world of men, "That little threshing-floor

64

which makes men so contentious." The clean of heart can say with Emerson: "The secret of virtue is to know that the richer another is the richer am I." [4a]

Does all this sound remote, vague, ethereal? So did it sound to Dante when first he heard of the riches that, the more distributed, the more increase the wealth of the individual. We, too, may be earth-bound, buried in material concerns and anxieties, intent—and in the conditions of modern life necessarily so—on installing a new heating unit, buying shoes for the baby, building a garage and keeping up payments on life insurance. More tragically, we may be ardent in keeping up with the Joneses, in asserting our real or fancied rights, untiring in the chase after power and prestige and so shortsighted even in our devotion to the things of the spirit that we perpetually mistake means for ends and yield stultifying loyalty to mechanical routines, narrow partisanship and the sectarian mentality. Or else we may be like the man who makes formal profession of indifference to worldly wealth and yet spends most of his days feverishly accumulating money, or the man who declares that matter does not exist at all and makes a fortune in the real-estate market. The Temple of the Spirit must indeed seem an unsubstantial fabric to the worshiper in the Temple of Mammon.

What is the logical, sensible attitude toward worldly wealth? Since, as the saying goes, you can't take it with you, wealth dominated by the quantitative standard—the riches that cannot be shared without corresponding diminution—has but a minor and secondary importance. Seek first the king-

[4a] *Letters to a Friend*, p. 27.

dom of the spirit, the world of the imponderables. The saint, the thinker, the artist lays up treasures in heaven; but likewise he usually contrives to eat regularly and to live on the average as long as the plutocrat, the sensualist and the demagogue. An idealist can be realistic. He can be in the world but not of it. He can, in the kindest sense of the phrase, make the best of both worlds. He can drive Brother Ass without letting Brother Ass drive him. He can, in short, exercise detachment from material things.

We have not here a lasting city. The artist knows that as well as the philosopher and the saint. So he eats what is set before him—though not always all of it—and he wears a rogue shirt in due season, and when he has occasion to travel he contemns not the invention of the late George Pullman. All the time, however, the deepest and truest part of him is in love with spiritual things. He refuses to gain the world and lose his soul. He is nonattached to the material wealth that passes through his hands, to prevailing standards of living, to the ebb and flow of economic, social and political movements, to the needs of his body, to the demands of his class or rank, to the putrescent glamour of fame. His feet are on the solid earth, but his forehead bumps the stars.

If the logical consequences of the priority of spiritual values appear tenuous and impractical it is not because the Temple of the Spirit is a castle in the clouds; it is because the material world is too much with us. Earnest college instructors used to bewail the overemphasis on athletics in the Grove of Academe. They did not utterly condemn games and physical exercise; they merely insisted that first things

66

should be first, that, as Woodrow Wilson once reminded the sports-mad alumni of Princeton, the side show is not the main tent. So, in stressing the priority of spiritual values, we are not denying the existence of material values nor repudiating the legitimate use of them; we are merely insisting that they should be kept in their place, which is not first place. Because their demands are obvious, unceasing and imperative, material values are liable to tyrannize over our thoughts and our lives. Easily, imperceptibly, even those of us who profess dedication to things spiritual can become enslaved to the flesh and the lusts thereof, to anger and envy, to pride and greed; and, especially, to sloth.

Sloth is in some respects the most subtle and disruptive of the Seven Deadly Sins. Contrary to popular assumption, sloth is not exclusively or chiefly physical inertia, sluggishness, malingering, "laying down on the job." In that sense, particularly in our strenuous epoch, when the gospel of hustle and high pressure is preached and practiced, sloth is comparatively rare and encounters social disapproval. A man may say, "I am as lazy as I can afford to be," but in the pursuit of material goods he can't afford to be lazy. In the pursuit of spiritual goods, however, the goods that can be shared without diminution, sloth is widespread and tacitly condoned. Witness the tedium of the tired businessman at the opera, the languor of the successful lawyer as he is dragged through the Louvre, the sullen boredom of the egotistic automobile salesman at a performance of *Othello*. Observe the general lack of relish for any but the least demanding poetry, the common disregard of philosophic reading and thinking, the passive acceptance of religion only as a Sunday soporific. Sluggishness in spiritual effort is the most prevalent of the capital vices, conspicuous in the psychology of the crowd and

L'error dei ciechi che si fanno duci,[5]

the mistake of the blind who make themselves leaders. *Acedia,* sloth in the field of the imponderables, and its resulting unrest and dissatisfaction, is defined by Aquinas as "a certain sadness by which man is made slow to spiritual acts," and "grief because of apparent evil which is real good." [6] It begets that weariness in well-doing which clouds our perception of spiritual reality. It causes us to take the imponderables sadly, or flippantly, not seriously.

The clean of heart need not and should not run to the extremes of detachment from material things advocated by sundry flint-souled fanatics of the East and of the West. Epictetus, for all his essential nobility, was hardly fair to Brother Ass: "I stuff this sack, and then I empty it again. What is more troublesome?" Behind many of the traditional fulminations against gluttony and lust there would seem to lie the blasphemous conviction that the Creator blundered in endowing man with animal needs and instincts, that food and drink are indecent and degrading, that there ought to be some way of perpetuating the human race other than by copulation. All that may indeed indicate detachment from material things, but it is a morbid fixation, a phobia as un-

---

[5] *Purgatorio,* xviii, 18.
[6] *Summa Theologica,* Prima, lxii, 2, and Secunda, xxxv, 1.

wholesome and unholy as the monomania of the degenerate.

Asceticism is a worthy ideal. It makes for sanity, balance, temperance in the regulation of our physical needs and appetites. It is a technique of "keeping fit" with a view to both our animal and spiritual nature. It is the athletic ideal applied to the complete man. But, just as athleticism frequently degenerates into the brute force and fakery of the "rassler" and the plug-ugly, so asceticism can develop into an inhuman, perverse, muscle-bound masochism. Enlightened masters of the spiritual life view the excesses of asceticism with the suspicion born of experience. They discourage the neophyte from pounding his breast with a stone, scourging himself with razor blades, starving himself into chronic invalidism and concomitant bad temper, and making self-discipline an extravaganza of competitive fanaticism. They know that self-discipline lies in the faithful and cheerful performance of daily duties, in a respectful regard for the comfort and preferences of other people, in the effort to garner the fair fruits of happiness, serenity and brotherly love. Why should a man detach himself from a hair-do and attach himself to a hair shirt?

Nonattachment is mainly a matter of mental and emotional self-control. A man is detached from food and drink, for example, when he gives but passing thought and slight affection to food and drink, not when he sprinkles sand on his spinach and pours vinegar into his tea. A man is detached from the lusts of the flesh when he regulates his sensual nature in harmony with an approved code of conduct and in accordance with the conviction that his body is the dwelling place of the Holy Spirit, not when he spends hours and days fighting self-induced temptations and forgets that, as Piers Plowman put it, the uncharitable chaste shall howl in hell. A man is detached from money when he earns it honestly, uses it prudently and unostentatiously and thinks about it as little as he can, not when he vows never to touch the filthy stuff and smothers his less heroic fellow mortals under a blanket condemnation.

More insidious than the lust of the flesh is the lust for power, dignity, prestige and social approbation. To live one's life and do one's work, it is ordinarily preferable to cooperate with other people rather than to antagonize them, and the realization that they esteem and respect us is cheering and encouraging. But we can fall imperceptibly into attachment to praise, applause and commendation. We come to seek social approval, to trim our sails to catch the anesthetic breeze of flattery, to grieve when it veers away from us. To the man of vital temperament it is always a trial to be at odds with the crowd; yet, if he is doing anything worth while, he might as well realize that it is impossible to please everybody all the time and that *mobile vulgus* is unaccountably and capriciously mobile. I hold in no special esteem the Athenian orator who, when the crowd burst into applause, remarked *sotto voce*, "I must have said something foolish"; but he was more admirable than the modern leader who estimates his importance by the volume of his fan mail. Blessed is the man who can be serenely indifferent to both censure and commendation, accepting both with urbane grace and deriving whatever benefit he can from each, yet living his life and doing his work regardless of praise or blame.

All power is corrupting, Lord Acton declared, and absolute power is absolutely corrupting. Nothing fails like success, for nothing is more intoxicating than the exercise of dominion over others. Drunken, though not with wine, are tyrannical teachers, possessive parents, dictatorial office managers, pontifical psychoanalysts, supercilious ticket sellers at the theater and functionaries of high and low degree who assume the role of indispensable man. And truly pathetic is the case of those who are so attached to their office of authority that severance from it means a depletion and impoverishment of their essential lives. Addiction to notoriety and the display of authority is more degrading than addiction to opium and alcohol. The disintegration it works on human personality is usually irreparable. Only with difficulty does the officeholder succeed in following the truth whithersoever it leads.

The disinterested pursuit of the imponderables is equally difficult for the fervent disciple who attaches himself wholly and unreservedly to a party, a coterie, an institution or a group. Gustave Le Bon in *The Psychology of the Crowd,* and before him Henry George in *Progress and Poverty,* called attention to the significant fact that the crowd mentality—something other than the sum of the individual mentalities composing the crowd—lags behind individuals in honesty, industry, clearness of thought and nobility of purpose. The boy in his gang will do things unworthy of his personal habits and good breeding; the man in a lynching mob gives way to an

71

emotional orgy he would repudiate in his individual daily life; the head of a state will countenance persons and practices he would not tolerate as head of a family.

Groups of all sizes, whether political, educational, ecclesiastical, artistic or social, have their value—often immense—in spurring on the indolent and giving a sense of security and importance to the mediocre among their members; but the groups may at the same time gravely handicap their more brilliant, aggressive and idealistic members who almost certainly will not invariably hew to the party line. Then for the individual comes a clash of loyalties which too often he solves through the formula, "Right or wrong, my country!" The proper solution, of course, is not to do away with groups, but to accept them for what they are, to understand their composite psychology, to utilize their resources when practicable and to ignore them when they are manifestly at variance with higher and more catholic conceptions of truth, beauty and goodness. This the spirit of blind and narrow partisanship simply cannot achieve. Hence the need of nonattachment to a group, no matter how popular and powerful, how admirable, how traditionally sanctioned. What doth it profit a man to gain the group and lose his soul?

Toward the end of his *Republic* Plato sets down, in words attributed to Socrates, the animating aims of detachment from the good which cannot be shared without loss. The souls of all men are given their choice of their status in a future life. One selects the career of a ruler, another a life of wealth and luxury, and so on. Last of all comes the soul of Odysseus, wise and disillusioned, indifferent to power and riches and ambition, and he gladly chooses what everybody else has rejected, the life of an obscure citizen without responsibility and prestige. More than two thousand years later the cryptic poet, Gerard Manley Hopkins, wrote, and not at all cryptically, "It is the holier lot to be unknown than to be known."

Somewhere along the path that leads to the Temple of the Spirit the wayfarer meets a soul sentinel who asks, Have you anything to declare? Do you confess to addiction to intemperance and violence, to fraud and greed? Are you conscious of envy and pride? Have you given more thought than needful to the goods which cannot be shared? Have you so attached yourself to means and systems and institutions that you have blinded your eyes to present realities and ultimate ends? Have you mistaken the symbol for the thing, the shadow for the substance? Have you fallen short of universal, unprovincial interests and aims? Have you allowed your self-will to blot out the splendor of the living God? Not until you have made your declaration may you join the company of the clean of heart.

V AS WE ARE IN TRUTH

Who enters here leaves pride behind is the inscription carved above the portals of the Temple of the Spirit. Without exception, masters of the spiritual life have preached humility; without exception, men and women who have won to spiritual insight have practiced humility. Gautama Buddha found the way of lowliness to be the path to wisdom. Saint Paul, by natural temperament no shrinking and self-effacing soul, styled himself the least of the Apostles. From his Oxford days John Wesley exemplified the humble heart which his brother Charles celebrated in sacred song. "I am what I am in the sight of God, and that is all," declared the Little Man of Assisi, and he wished his followers to be known as the Friars Minor. Striking but deeply symbolical was the conduct of Saint Peter Celestine. Chosen Pope, he found the lavishly furnished palace so repugnant to his tastes that in one of the vast chambers he constructed a tiny cell where he lived apart from pomp and splendor. His humility even led him to resign his exalted office. He realized in his lowly preferences the ideal formulated by Christ: "I am in the midst of you as one that serveth." Traditionally the wearers of the papal tiara sign themselves "the servant of the servants of God."

If the word humility makes us uncomfortable, it may be that we are victims of an unreasoning aversion to certain words; or else we misconceive the meaning of humility. Perhaps we associate humility with Dickens's Uriah Heep, who rubbed his slimy hands and protested that he was "so 'umble." We forgot the classical definition of humility: Knowledge of ourselves as we are in truth. Acceptance of the Greek admonition, Know thyself, leads inevitably to the Christian—and Hebrew—conception of humility. The man who knows himself can confess with Hamlet: "I am myself indifferent honest; but yet I could accuse me of such things that it were better my mother had not borne me."

Dwellers in the world of the imponderables are sometimes accused of exaggeration and affectation in minimizing their accomplishments and placing a low estimate on their character. But they see things *sub specie aeternitatis*, they take the long-range view. They reach after an exalted, indeed an impossible, ideal of perfection; they are intent upon what Matthew Arnold called a high and flawless excellence. Flaubert was humble in his quest of the one noun to designate an object, the one verb to animate it, the one adjective to convey its shape and color. Alfred de Musset was humble when he sighed, "It takes a great deal of life to make a little art." For when a man holds fast to spiritual values he becomes acutely conscious of the puniness of his powers, the inadequacy of his skills. His language is repugnant and incomprehensible to the man who esteems only externals, whose purpose is to keep up appearances, who basks in the approval

76

of *mobile vulgus,* who assumes that the art of arts it to "get by."

Not only in the religious field is humility of heart held in reverence. Eminent musicians and artists, thinkers and writers, have had, like all of us, their vanities and their egotisms, but for the most part, and because their knowledge of spiritual reality was profound, they manifested in one way or another that divine discontent and self-disparagement which Newton voiced when he saw himself as a child walking beside the sea and picking up a handful of the shells and pebbles of knowledge. "All I know," declared the philosopher-saint Aquinas, "I have learned at the foot of the crucifix." It is related of the same *Doctor Angelicus* that when he was reading aloud in the refectory and one of his brethren—a type discoverable in any community—"corrected" him on the pronunciation of a word, Thomas violated a Latin quantity rather than violate fraternal charity. By nature a proud and impatient man, and a man not loath to recognize his own worth, Dante Alighieri yet girded himself with the reed of meekness before ascending the Purgatorial Mountain, and was almost excessive in his self-depreciation when praising other great men—Virgil, his teacher and his guide, Aristotle, "the master of those who know." It is freely granted that the humility of artists, poets and musicians, like the humility of saints, did not usually extend into every phase of living and every department of social intercourse, but it did color their attitude toward their specific arts. It did, that is, when they were really great artists; the smaller fry are likely to pray with the mythical Scotsman, "God gie us a guid conceit of oursels."

"The higher we are placed the more humbly should we walk." Truly great men are truly humble men; and their humility is the real thing. It goes deeper and further than modesty. It is not "humility with a hook"—self-denigration calculated to bring down a shower of reassuring eulogiums. Humility springs from knowledge of self, not from ignorance of self. The very human canine protagonist in Miss G. B. Stern's *The Ugly Dachshund* was not humble; he simply didn't know what kind of dog he was. He was unusual only in this, that he thought he was a dachshund when in reality he was a great Dane, whereas most victims of self-ignorance think they are great Danes when they are only dachshunds —and not the most endearing specimens of the breed. Nor should humility be confused with diffidence, spinelessness, timidity or what Horace Fletcher labeled "fearthought," a "self-suggestion of inferiority." The humble man is not a reed shaken by the wind; the meek *shall* inherit the earth! Your humble soul may be tender-hearted, but he must be tough-minded; notably difficult to override, he is by no means what Emerson called a mush of concession.

There can be, as we read in *The Table-Talk of John Selden, humilitas quaedam in vitio,* for human nature is prone to concur in William Blake's belief that the road of excess leads to the palace of wisdom. Selden judiciously observes that "if a man hath too mean an opinion of himself, 'twill render him unserviceable both to God and man." But that is largely an academic consideration: "Humility is a virtue all preach, none practice," and therefore scarcely carry to extremes. Theorists have drawn up degrees of humility, the highest— or lowest—of which is deliberately and actively to seek reprobation and contempt. That ultimate degree of humility Selden must have had in mind when he said none practice it. As the Irish priest explained in another connection: "For the same man to preach and to practice is an unfair division of labor."

A man can be humble of heart without having ever heard about degrees of humility. Every college has its distinguished scholar and constructive teacher who is unassuming in his bearing, circumspect in his opinions, humorously unimpressed by his academic degrees—his union cards he may call them—gently contemptuous of academic flummery and aloof from the swirling currents of campus politics and the low cunning of his male spinster associates. If biographers and gossipmongers have underlined the vanities and foibles of illustrious men, it may be because of an abnormally keen nose for diverting news; the journalistic approach finds a newsworthy contrast between a man's eccentricities and his habitual conduct and character. Genius has been known to praise itself for humorous effect. Whistler's "Why drag in Velasquez?" was comical to him as to us. When Thackeray, on completing a famous scene in *Vanity Fair*, slapped his thigh and exclaimed, "By Jove, that's a stroke of genius!" we may suspect that he sought diversion in a bit of innocuous clowning; prevailingly he did not have a good conceit of himself.

Sometimes what looks on the surface like vanity is really

79

an up-surging of humility. On one occasion John Drew, having read a highly complimentary comment on his acting, was so frankly delighted that he wore a clipping into shreds showing it to acquaintances in clubs and hotel lobbies. Vanity? Superficially, perhaps. But let it be remembered that John Drew then stood at the pinnacle of his career and was undisputed head of his profession. He had only to flap his elbows and rub his chin to convince audiences that he was a great actor. The fact that he was so pleased with the review in a comparatively obscure magazine would seem to indicate that he had no strong assurance of his own worth. Basically he was a humble man.

Preachers and moralists have roughly handled the Pharisee who stood up in the temple and thanked God that he was not as the rest of men. He lived a good life. He shunned the commoner vices, he gave himself to ascetic exercises, he said his prayers; and he was not unmindful of his brethren in distress. The only thing wrong with him was, not his virtue, but his complacent contemplation of his virtue. He was good and he knew it. He lacked humility. His self-knowledge was not all-inclusive. He would have crouched down beside the despised publican had he the spiritual courage to recall his shortcomings. He did well when he thanked the Lord for helping him to obey the Commandments; he would have done better had he asked forgiveness for his sins against the Commandments. Like so many of us in every age, the Pharisee had developed the knack of overlooking his defects, his stupidities, his petty meannesses, his waywardness, his unjust estimates of his fellows. Mrs. Pharisee, I am sure, could have suggested a few things for him to think about. It never occurred to him to soliloquize thus: "Here I've lived for half a century, and on the whole I'm a pretty poor specimen of a man. I've made countless mistakes. I've been thoughtless and cruel and unkind, I've passed snap judgments on the motives of other men, and over and over I've made a frightful fool of myself. I give Thee thanks, O Lord, that because of Thy mercies, I am not a bigger ass than I am."

Many of us condemn the Pharisee; but we make him our patron saint. We cultivate an unwarranted good conceit of ourselves. We conveniently forget our perversities and peccadilloes. We attribute our graver sins to the manly imperiousness of our warm oriental nature. We favor books and lectures and sermons which flatter our smugness. We can't see how often we talk nonsense, are vindictive and unjust, stand helpless under the attack of passion—anger and envy, greed and lust. It never occurs to us that at times, in doing good, in defending fine ideals, in cleaving to right ideas, we offend against charity and seemliness and truth.

In recent years there has arisen a cult of corporate humility, an absorption in the weaknesses and limitations of humanity in general. We speak pityingly of the little people and rail at the folly of nationalism and the insanity of war. We piously shake our heads over "poor human nature." We give eager assent to the eloquent summation made by Mr. Bertrand Russell in *A Free Man's Worship:* "Brief and powerless is man's life; on him and all his race the slow, sure doom falls pitiless and dark."

But corporate humility will not do. All this whining over

the woes and weaknesses of humanity is but a suppuration from the festering sores of individual complacency and pride. It echoes not Saint Francis but the Pharisee. It is as easy— and as useless—to pity humanity in general as it is to love humanity in general. It reminds me of a communist speaker I heard one Sunday afternoon in London's Hyde Park. He was without exception the ablest orator I have ever listened to. He held his heterogeneous audience entranced. He made them laugh and he made them weep. He stirred them to anger and persuaded them to action. And then he revealed his inadequate philosophy of life: "I despise you, I hate you —you and you and you! As individuals you disgust me, you turn my stomach, you bore me to death. But for humanity I'd cheerfully lay down my life." Was that speaker a humble man?

If corporate humility is a delusion, corporate pride is a snare. Plenty of people will be slow in word or thought to dwell on their individual excellences, real or imagined; but let them belong to a group or class or coterie and they become offensively bumptious and blatant in voicing pride in the association. The Cabots speak only to Lowells. The alumnus of good old Siwash knows himself to be several cuts above the graduate of Saint Homobonus. Shining superiority is conferred through membership in the swank and exclusive Mudhen Club. Some years ago the public relations office of a religious denomination pointed out that *Who's Who in America* listed proportionately more members of that sect than of any other—as though the function of a religious organization were to shepherd the socially, financially and intellectually prominent. Monks have been known to forget all they ever knew about humility when defending the prestige of "our holy order." Corporate pride expresses itself in shallow broadmindedness and intolerable tolerance, but most of all in unrestrained nationalism. As Mr. Aldous Huxley has aptly said,

> Thus, all "God's Englishmen" are superior to "the lesser breeds without the law" and every individual God's-English-man is entitled to think himself superior to every member of the lesser breed, even the lordliest and wealthiest, even the most intelligent, the most highly gifted, the most saintly. Any man who believes strongly enough in the local nationalistic idolatry can find in his faith an antidote against even the most acute inferiority complex. Dictators feed the flames of national vanity and reap their reward in the gratitude of millions to whom the conviction that they are participants in the glory of the divine nation brings relief from the gnawing consciousness of poverty, social unimportance and personal insignificance.[1]

Corporate pride in creed or college, in race or social class, is commonly justified as an expression of commendable loyalty. But vice is vicious, irrespective of the source that feeds it. Money-madness, for instance, is odious whether the dollar-chaser is intent on filling his personal purse or financing a hospital for crippled children. In either case he will develop bad manners, make a nuisance of himself, disrupt his sense of proportion, flatter his wealthy fellow citizens and coarsen and degrade his soul through excessive immer-

[1] *Ends and Means,* pp. 109-110. © 1937 by the author. Published by Harper & Brothers.

sion in material interests. Even a laudable end does not justify an immoral means. Similarly, pride is pride, even when generated by the virtue of loyalty, and bears the gravely malignant fruits of pride. Though it fly the flag of heaven it is still the sin whereby the angels fell.

In its specific meaning, pride is undue satisfaction taken in a quality or an accomplishment solid and substantial. Pride of intellect is found only in men of intellect. A scholar may be proud of his linguistic attainments, a scientist of his contributions to chemistry or aerodynamics. An undoubted savant, however basically uneducated, was the professor who always took off his hat when he mentioned his own name. Vanity, as distinguished from pride, is overcomplacency on account of traits or deeds comparatively trivial. A man is vain when he puffs and struts because he becomingly wears Bond Street clothes or at sixty still has a full head of hair. A woman is vain when she preens herself on the fact that in middle age she displays a perfect thirty-six whilst her less fortunate sisters flounder in a floating forty-eight. The proverb, "Pride may be found in the Capuchin's beard," really commemorates vanity; members of the Capuchin branch of the Franciscan order wear beards, and the friar inordinately conscious of his hirsute glory is vain rather than proud.

We take pride in something big, we are vain of something little, and we are conceited simply because—Saint Francis in reverse—we are what we are. I have visited Perugia, therefore Perugia is an interesting town; but Orvieto, because I have never been there, is a negligible place. I am five feet, nine inches tall; Jones is a dwarf, only five feet four, and

Smith is a giant, six feet two. The Strollers Club, of which I am a charter member, has tone and influence; the rival Ramblers Club is the last refuge of roughnecks. I don't care what the dictionary says, I pronounce *exquisite* with the accent on the *quiz* and *hospitable* with the accent on the *pit*. And, since I am living in it, the twentieth century is the most enlightened, the most progressive, the most illustrious of the centuries. Conceit is personal provincialism, spiritual myopia. It is contentment carried to ridiculous excess—smugness and overblown complacency.

Some shortsighted parents look with disfavor on the inculcation of a salutary humility in child training. They fear that even a moderate discipline in decency, decorum and respect for the rights and dignity of adults will break the spirit of their offspring. So they coddle their children and encourage them to develop into odious little brats. One such father said the other day: "I want my son to learn how to make his way in the world. I want him to get ahead and keep ahead, to be aggressive and self-assertive. It's a tough pace, and he'll lose out unless he has lots of drive and self-assurance."

It did not occur to that gentleman that self-importance and self-assurance have sent more boys to the devil or the penitentiary than to God or the seats of the mighty. The "damn my eye" outlook, nurtured in snob schools and smart sets, breeds no clear-seeing watchers of the skies. Drive and self-assurance, exalted into predatory nationalism, hurled us into two world wars within a quarter of a century—conflicts which conceivably could have been avoided had our politicians and publicists, our financiers and demagogues learned

85

in their school days to be meek and humble of heart. Old and young have failed to ask themselves with Montaigne, "What do I know?"

The qualities which facilitate success in any field of legitimate human activity—intelligence, awareness, patience, courage, perseverance—are not incompatible with humility. In business and professional life self-knowledge is a potent asset; but in the realm of the imponderables it is indispensable. Devoid of humility, we not only lag and falter on the way to the Temple of the Spirit; our eyes are blinded to the supreme and abiding realities. The humble of heart develop resistance against spiritual bacteria. They rarely follow false lights or draw conclusions based on what Coleridge termed "quasific and mendicant premises." They offer fewer and slighter obstacles to the flow of divine influences into their souls. Because they are relatively free of narrow self-interest, they let their light shine before men—and remain indifferent to its shining. Like Browning's Pippa and Hawthorne's David Swan, they are unknowing instruments of grace and illumination. Theirs is "the hearing ear, the understanding heart."

Narrow the gate of humility may be, but strait also is the way. In many instances the humble of heart gain entrance into the Temple of the Spirit without prolonged and weary wanderings in the dark forest of uncertainty and unrest. On the other hand, pride and conceit impede the spiritual advancement of many an otherwise noble and generous soul. Eventually such persons arrive at a perception of the imponderables and win to participation in the order of the spiritual world. It is somewhat the fashion to assume that because they were so long in finding their way they must be exceptionally robust characters. Occasionally they themselves admit the soft impeachment. Of eleventh-hour neophytes John Campbell Shairp wrote words pertinent and timely still:

> Let none, therefore, pride themselves on having doubts and uncertainties on religious subjects, as if it were a fine thing to have them, proving them to be intellectual athletes, and entitling them to look down on those who are free from them as inferior persons, less mentally gifted. For there is a higher state than their own—there is a purer atmosphere, which has been breathed by persons of as strong intellect as themselves, but of a finer spirit. . . . For the spirit of a man is a very delicate instrument, which, if it be distorted out of its natural courses, this way or that, by prejudice or interest or double-dealing on the one hand, or foolhardiness and self-confidence on the other, may never perhaps in this life recover its equilibrium.[2]

Precious are the treasures of the humble. One of them is immunity from a foolish consistency, Emerson's "hobgoblin of little minds." Self-knowledge induces growth, growth is a form of change, and change of any sort the proud man condemns as inconsistent. "It's too late now," a fighting editor said when shown that his vitriolic attack on a public man was unjustified; "I've started this thing and I'm going to finish it." Conceit not less than cunning animates the ward-heeler wisdom embodied in the motto, "When you make a mistake

[2] "Hindrances to Spiritual Growth," *Great Essays* (Aldine Edition), pp. 383-384.

try to correct it, but never admit you've been wrong." Humility suggests a more manly course, illustrated by Mr. Van Wyck Brooks. Like so many Americans of his generation, he wrote before he was ripe, conducted his education in public:

> My early writings won a few adherents, who were less mature even than I was, and they still say and write that I have gone back on myself when I have only gone back on my ignorance and brashness.[3]

Ignorance the humble man acknowledges, brashness he speedily sheds.

Humility likewise facilitates escape from the drag of fad and fashion and the modish shibboleths of the hour. It counteracts what Mr. Powys calls "our pathetic docility towards a vulgarized public opinion" and "the insidious hypnosis of custom." It keeps a man from wincing when he is branded a Victorian in literature, a Pre-Raphaelite in art, a medievalist in religion. Self-knowledge leads a thinker to see that the easy trick of tacking labels on modes of thought is frequently nothing more than a substitute for dynamic thinking. And it makes no difference at all. Call him a Pelagian or a Probabilist, a Futurist or a Primitive, a Gongorist or a Ciceronian, you fail to ruffle the equanimity of the humble man. He declines to live by tags rather than by truths. And he is but slightly responsive to the shows of scholarship which so often conceal a dearth of substance; the academic whited sepulcher is crammed with dead men's bones.

[3] *Opinions of Oliver Allston,* p. 27. © 1941 by the author. Published by E. P. Dutton & Co., Inc.

He that would find his life must lose it. He loses it, not in a dark room fumbling for something that isn't there, not in amateur philosophy or homemade theology or rule-of-thumb aesthetics, not in the dismal slough of negation and futility or the whirlpool of vague and blundering benevolence which whips its victims into the tragic impertinence of molding the world nearer to their shallow hearts' desire. The humble man loses himself in something higher and finer and greater than himself. He clings to the nobler hypothesis. Aware of his own stupidity, he sits at the feet of the world's supreme thinkers, and he is courteous enough and intelligent enough to hear them out before attempting to evaluate their teachings. Admitting his own entanglement in temporal and material concerns, he wins to enrichment and freedom by forgetting himself in music, poetry and art. Conscious of his moral deficiencies and his limited spiritual discernment, he bows his head within the Temple of the Spirit where Power and Love and Wisdom speak with eternal resonance. He welcomes the advice of Francis Quarles: "In the meditation of divine mysteries keep thy heart humble. The best way to see daylight is to put thy candle out."

VI EVERY MAN'S A MONK

On a California hillside which he perversely spelled "The Hights," a poet who looked like Walt Whitman spent the second half of a long life. Much of the time he was alone. No scholar, he had but a handful of books; no devotee of systematic desk work, he wrote little. Booted and hatted, he whiled away hours on a bearskin-draped couch, gazing out on the oaks and madrones and down upon the city of Oakland and steel-gray San Francisco Bay. He puttered about his rambling house, even installing perforated pipes to simulate rain on the roof during the dry season. Here and there on the estate he piled up rock monuments to Moses and other men he delighted to honor. He saluted visitors gruffly, but soon thawed out into genial conversation, discoursing of the writer's craft, of civilization, of immortality—"Certainly I believe in a future life, but not for everybody; some men are too rotten to live after they die"—interspersing reminiscences of his youth among the Oregon Indians and his picturesque incursions into London drawing rooms. And sooner or later he would proclaim his *apologia*—in terms the reverse of apologetic—for living on "The Hights": "You've got to get away from things if you really want to see them. The breath of life is not in cities; it's on the hilltops and the sea. Up here I'm alive. Down there on the cement sidewalks I'd be only another walking corpse in a clabber of dead men."

Joaquin Miller was an eccentric, of course, even an inoffensively conscious eccentric; and I am sure he would have sullied the clean air with colorful profanity had anybody told him that he was approximating to the monastic ideal. Yet it was the embryo monk in the minor poet that responded to the sunlit seclusion of "The Hights." Beneath the posing and the tall tales, the homespun philosophy and the protective brusqueness, there was something fine and deep in Joaquin Miller. To him that remote hillside was a site for the Temple of the Spirit. His motives in living from the crowd apart, though less comprehensive and exalted than the ideals that inspired Saint Benedict at Subiaco and the Abbé de Rancé at La Trappe, were not entirely alien to the motives which once dotted the Egyptian desert with hermits and reared monastic piles on Monte Cassino and in the Valley of Chartreuse.

Chesterton maintained that every man is monogamous, even if he is monogamous only for a month. Similarly, every man is a monk, even if his monastic tenure is brief and broken and his hermitage is only a modern bathroom. Despise not the bathroom, by the way; it is the only place in a city apartment where solitude is assured.

Artists and writers understand the necessity of seclusion as fully as saints and seers. Cicero had as many as eight houses of retreat, notably his villa at Tusculum above Frascati, whence to look down upon the Campagna and ripen his reflections on the imponderables. Horace had his Sabine

Farm to restore his sense of proportion after periodic visits
to the Roman Forum. Petrarca found in his modest château
at Vaucluse beside the roaring Sorgues an invigorating
change from the teeming streets of papal Avignon. Balzac
maintained hideouts in Paris where he meditated and wrote
and whence he emerged unshaven and emaciated. Turner,
the English painter, sought and found the soul in his sunsets
by living incognito in Chelsea, where the neighbors knew
him as Admiral Booth. Even so vital an extrovert as Sir
Walter Scott, lavish of hospitality and rich in human juices,
fled now and then from his baronial Abbotsford when over-
taxed by what Lockhart describes as "the solemn applauses
of learned dulness, the vapid raptures of painted and peri-
wigged dowagers, the horseleech avidity with which under-
bred foreigners urged their questions, and the pompous sim-
pers of condescending magnates."

By temperament and preference anything but an anchor-
ite, Lord Byron welcomed seasons of seclusion. For months
he lived and wrote in an island monastery near Venice. Practically every artist worth his salt dreams of a stone tower fac-
ing the sea or a clapboard shack among the pines where he
can ruminate and concentrate and search his soul. Even the
fabulous tired businessman toys with the project of a chicken
run in Georgia, an out-of-the-way New England farm, a
walled garden in Pasadena, a private island in the English
Channel, the South Seas or off the coast of Mexico. Invariably castles in Spain have a monastic aura.

The institution of monasticism supplies a vital human need,
a need felt at times even by men and women who love the

world and the vanities thereof. We are all gregarious animals, obviously; but just as obviously each one of us is a lone wolf. "I dislike to leave Paris," said Joubert, "for that means separation from my friends; and I dislike to leave the country, for that means separation from myself."

The monk, simply and practically, is a man who sacrifices society for solitude. Naturally he can overdo it and illustrate the dictum that it is not good for man to be alone. Anchorites, literal and complete, nowadays are few, and the strictly eremitical way of life is encouraged by neither church nor state. In its insistence on community life monasticism concedes some play to the social instinct, and it furnishes incentives to solitude through prescribed periods for silence and meditation, prayer and study. When, as sometimes has happened, it falls conspicuously short of its ideals, monasticism can become a scandal and a reproach; but at its best it offers a helpful and congenial ambient for dedication to God and the life of the spirit to artists and poets, scholars and saints. Obviously the monastic life is not for every man; but every man has something of the monk in him, because, in whatever degree, he hungers and thirsts after the imponderables. He knows, if he knows anything spiritual at all, that on his journey to the Temple of the Spirit he travels fastest who travels alone. The Lord is not in the wind, the Lord is not in the tempest.

Aware of his frailty and instability, the monk binds himself by sacred promises to his chosen way of life. Men who by reason of temperament or domestic obligations or repug-

94

nance to what they consider extremism, decline to follow the rigidly monastic way can find a modified form of it in the retreat. During a month or a week or a week end the retreatments live in a monastic environment, observe regular hours, keep away from newspapers and radios, immure themselves from visitors and telephone calls, follow a schedule of reading and instruction, meditation and prayer.

Long ago the American novelist, F. Marion Crawford, pointed out that the retreat idea could and should be adopted by persons wishing to get the best from literature, and he might have included patrons of music and the arts. University summer sessions and writers' conventions utilize at least a few of the monastic practices. To shut out the distractions of daily life, to forget about money, family and neighbors the better to breathe a nonmaterial air and renew one's faith in spiritual entities—that is in a measure the monastic ideal and wins response from the lone-wolf strand in our complex human nature. And the prime essential of it is solitude.[1]

In society we give; in solitude we grow. By the side of a country road is a well of water cool and soft and sweet; often of evenings motorists come to it with pails and jugs, and they can see the water sparkling in the shadowed depths. What they cannot see are the sources of that refreshing flow

[1] In the exact and canonical meaning of the word, the monk or religious is such because he makes vows of poverty, chastity and obedience in an order, congregation or institute approved by the Church. In the text we are concerned with the psychological need of solitude experienced by every man who gets beneath the surface of life at all. Monks are technically professionals in withdrawal from the world, even though some of them may be less adept in the practice of solitude than some amateurs.

—seepages from the surrounding rocks, rivulets on the lush hillsides, channels cut far beneath the surface of the earth. Let an earthquake come, or a real estate boom, to disrupt the unseen sources of the well, and the motorists would find their water supply impeded or destroyed. All that is a symbol of society and solitude. Normally we share with other human beings the fruitage of our thought and experience, our knowledge and our skill, our convictions and our intuitions. But we can do so effectively and continuously only when we cherish secret sources of replenishment and inspiration. Destroy the sources and you dry up the well. The only available substitute is the cistern, which has no sources of its own, which passively accepts anything poured or flung into it—from chlorine to dead cats—and which at best is but a container, a receptacle. The cistern personality depletes its resources; the well personality gives of its overflow.

One reason for the existence of cistern personalities is the difficulty many people experience in finding opportunities to withdraw into some sort of vivifying solitude. Ease of communication is not an unmixed blessing. It brings the world to our ears and our elbows, the world with its ephemeral interests, its fleeting enthusiasms, its meretricious standards of value. Especially must the city dweller realize the obstacles to inner withdrawal; solitude he finds in a dim church, maybe, or an unpopular alcove at the public library, among the Mayan collection at the museum or even in walking Fido on the broad sidewalks up by the Pacific Union Club. As Mr. Powys declares, "Gregariousness and a mania for society drag down, cheapen, vulgarize, the delicate and sensitive dignity of human life." [2]

Bodily health and mental vigor can exist in any climate, and solitude can be attained in any environment. That is theoretically true. But even as virility and genius flower most freely in temperate zones—William Gilpin's Isothermal Zodiac and Sir Halford Mackinder's Marginal Crescent—so the fruits of solitude are most readily realized in places unvexed by "the loud vociferations of the street." Environmental withdrawal tends to spiritual withdrawal, though not automatically producing it. For solitude can break a man as well as make him. It is possible, let us grant, to be in the world and not of it, to preserve inner solitude in the subway or on the Hoboken ferry, in New Orleans during Mardi Gras or on the Columbia when the salmon run begins. A friend of mine, a philosopher of sorts, indulges his normal monastic cravings by living each summer in Chicago's Loop. "Nobody knows me out there, and when I stroll along Madison Street I am utterly alone. I can think my own thoughts, be my own self. Distractions? I swat them like flies." Admiringly we dub him the Akund of Swat. Most of us find it hard to be solitary in a throng; the swatting is more distracting than the flies.

Fortunate is the seeker after solitude if his abode, seasonal or permanent, lies where tall trees point skyward and wild canaries dart about a colorful bird bath. A few books, mostly

[2] *A Philosophy of Solitude*, pp. 70-71. © 1933 by the author. By permission of Simon and Schuster, Inc.

time-tested ones, will help him too, and a radio or graphophone to bring him sweet sessions with Brahms or Tschaikowsky, the Prelude to *La Traviata,* the glorious second act of *Tannhäuser.* From the quiet walls the peace of a Luini Madonna or a sketch of temple ruins in Sicily will correct his mental perspective and restore his emotional balance. And all the better if his one-man dog dozes on the hearth-rug. Then may he exclaim with the strong-souled Saint Bernard: *"O Solitudo! O sola beatitudo!"*

Delivered from ticker tape and telephones, club luncheons and cocktail lounges, we enjoy immunity from both brickbats and bouquets. In our seasons of social activity, our periods of giving and sharing, we receive compliments and censures, a slap on the back, a knife in the ribs, and the knife is ordinarily less lethal than the slap. Both disturb our poise, confuse our judgment, dull our perceptions. Too much sociability, as insidious as the drug habit, changes our wells of immemorial wisdom into cisterns of shallow popular opinion. Obsessed with the here and now, and possessed by the devil of expediency, we blur our vision of timeless truth. Most compliments, like most censures, are ignorant and ill-advised. So it is salutary to slip out of the agora or the arena, to retire from the atmosphere of rootless thinking and modish bigotry, of sullen hostility and shifting approbation. Solitude clears the brain, steadies the soul. It washes out of us the spiritual parasites which breed and pululate in even the most admirable human assemblies. The banished Duke in *As You Like It* found tongues in trees, sermons in stones. Prospero in *The Tempest* had been a mediocre man and a fumbling administrator before he mastered his so-potent arts in sea-girt solitude.

The soldier in his foxhole sees little of the battle, has no adequate conception of the aims and progress of the campaign, and knows little or nothing concerning the issues of the war. He has to concentrate on his immediate and imperative job of killing and not being killed. Soldiers are we all in the foxholes of business and professional life. Our job, our manner of life, presses upon us claims, duties, obligations and patterns of thinking charged with the urgencies of the passing hour. That unceasing pressure prevents us from seeing life steadily and whole. Concentrating on means, we lose sight of ends. The group mentality claps the big end of the telescope to our eye, and far-off events appear more distant than divine. No soured misanthrope, but a clear-seeing and far-seeing psychologist, speaks in *The Imitation of Christ:* "As often as I have been among men I have come home less a man."

On the other hand, as the same writer said, "The cell continually dwelt in groweth sweet." Men intelligent and virile enough not to drift on the currents of campaign oratory and calculated propaganda, of human respect and treadmill activity, restore their sense of values in solitude—in a monk's cell or a trapper's cabin, on a fishing trip or a hike in the hills, on an ocean cruise devoid of deck games and dressing for dinner or in paddling on lake or river where every stroke generates more energy than it exhausts. The relief and restoration they experience is not merely the result of getting away from routine occupations and preoccupations; rather it is what happens to a man's vision when he looks at life with the small end of the telescope to his eye. In solitude comes a sharpening of perspective, a perception of the important and unimportant in custom and character, in amusement and enjoyment, in parasitic professions and constructive labors, in love and worship, in time and eternity. The momentous change in Tolstoy's philosophy of life, described in an eloquent passage in his *Confession*, was initiated one spring morning when he stood in the woods alone.

Like all doctors, oculists do not always see eye to eye, but a reputable group of them favor exercises whereby glasses are rendered unnecessary. One of the recommended methods of toning the eye muscles, shifting the focus, can easily be practiced by a man walking along a country road. At one moment he looks at his wrist watch, and then he scans the purpling hills; now he watches his dog chasing a rabbit, again he reads the license number of a passing car. In the course of an hour or two he has shifted the focus of vision thousands of times, exercising muscles all but unused in reading, filing a saw or tending a machine. He has rapidly alternated his gaze upon objects near and far, large and small, bright and obscure. He comes home, not less a man, but a better-seeing man.

Solitude all but compels us to shift our mental focus. The monk is not a monomaniac, and the man who spends a day, a month or a year in solitude is unlikely to dwell on one narrow topic all the time. He learns to shift his mental and spiritual vision. When he reads he is not a man of one book. He discovers that solitude seductively induces him to browse

100

intelligently and fruitfully, like the self-centered and fastidious goat as distinguished from the flock-conscious and undiscriminating sheep. Nothing that is human—or divine—need be foreign to him. He acquires a flexibility of interest while preserving an impregnable standard of taste. He doesn't have to talk, even to himself, about tolerance and fellowship and mutual understanding. Shifting the focus of his thoughts and emotions, he discerns the something good in the worst of us and the something bad in the best of us—in personalities and institutions, systems and theories. And he can relax, easing his tensions and refusing to worry over problems largely nonexistent or beyond his power to solve. In society we are like the office-worker straining his eyes and staring at columns of figures; in solitude we are like the stroller by the lake shifting the focus of vision from the haze-veiled mountains to the golden poppies at his feet, from the hawk watchfully soaring in the sky to the crane streaking low above the water.

One summer morning I was privileged to stand on the bridge of a cargo vessel shuttling from wharf to wharf in the Los Angeles harbor, and to listen to the pilot, trim and young and self-important, dilate on the hazards and burdens of his office. "You've got to have iron nerves," he assured me. "Everything's up to you. You never know what's going to happen. It makes a man old before his time. When we get to Terminal Island I'll be a rag." My ignorance, I fear, prevented me from being suitably impressed. Under other circumstances, bucking a heavy wind or groping through a fog, the pilot's task might indeed be exacting; but on that beaming day there appeared to be no nerve-shredding risk in guiding the *Rialto* down the narrow but uncongested channel.

Like the garrulous pilot, most of us take our work with deadly seriousness. And on the whole that is well. The man who empties a garbage pail or pulls a proof, paints a steeple or grooms a pup, manages a toy department or presides at a convention of philosophers puts more into his work and gets more out of it by persuading himself that his particular job is supremely significant and surcharged with possibilities and responsibilities. The waster as well as the worker feels like that at times. The man about town tripping to his tailor, the bore drifting from office to office to wear out chairs and patience, the flighty matron pouring tea and the gossip pouring poison are all galvanized by the conviction that their occupations are momentous and unique. Thus does gregariousness in work and play imperil our discernment of values, a discernment which only solitude can restore.

That harbor pilot would probably talk less and feel more deeply were he to cross the Western Ocean and through four weeks sight not a single sail. He might even get to thinking about the doldrums and the Southern Cross and "the trail that is always new." Certainly his scale of values would be expanded and renewed. So it is with all of us when we have the hardihood to break away from the throng. Power and pelf, fame and group approval are not nearly so important as we once fancied them to be. Things unseen weigh more than objects of shape and sense. We may even come to sense the triviality and impertinence of most human ambitions, and to see through galumphing poets, sport-spoiling prophets, fanatical saints and purblind seers. Words as words neither intoxicate nor antagonize us; we can't hear what people are saying, so we don't care what they say. We cast off provincialism like a suit of worn-out clothes. Perhaps a solitary sentry on the wall of Bethlehem one winter night was the only man in the crowded town who glimpsed unearthly radiance in a stable cave.

Like all good things, solitude can be abused, distorted and carried to wasteful and ridiculous excess. In large doses few men can take it. It can become a sentimental pose, an arid and debilitating routine, an artificial way of life. The spirit of solitude can be smothered in formalism, mechanical observance, fire-horse regularity; and it can degenerate into spiritual invalidism and emotional hypochondria. Even those readers who recognize Proust's gifts as a writer must agree that his withdrawal into the shadows and foul air of a sickroom had something unwholesome about it, that for all his virtuosity *A la recherche du temps perdu* lacks the zest, the vibrancy and the contagious feeling of abundant life which invariably characterize great literature, great music and great art. Like a sea voyage or a pack-in trip in the mountains, solitude, while exerting a tonic effect on some men, will only make others more petty and petulant. And always a shrine of solitude is menaced by those breezy bustling extroverts who bring the tumult and the shouting of the world within the holy place.

To cull the fruits of solitude we must turn to it freely and spontaneously. If we are dragooned into any kind of cloister, or enter one reluctantly and with misgivings, we might as well remain in the market place or on the battlefield. Nor should we adopt the way of solitude panoplied with charts and time tables of efficiency and progress. William James humorously and shrewdly warned his teacher audience at a lecture on "The Gospel of Relaxation": "Even now I fear that some of my fair hearers may be making an undying resolve to become strenuously relaxed." Solitude demands a quietism of sorts, a placid unconcern as to measurable and ponderable results, an easeful yielding to the spell and mood of the imponderables, like the unruffled calmness of the swimmer floating on the surface of the sea or of the little old woman sitting on her heels in the cool dimness of Siena's black and white marble duomo. In solitude the overesteemed fighting spirit has no place. If we don't like Rubinstein and *The Spiritual Exercises* of Saint Ignatius, there is no point in working ourselves into a passion of protest. Better to forget the Barcarolles and the Second Week, or else placidly and impersonally try to discover what other people find congenial in composer and saint.

Finally, solitude is denatured by a welter of rules and laws and regulations. One of the least estimable concomitants of monasticism is the community bell. It can be, as it has been piously called, the voice of God; also it can be a jangling irritation. While not subscribing to the Rabelaisian program *in toto* or acclaiming his fantastic Abbey of Theleme as an ideal of religious observance, we who turn to solitude for strength and growth and renewal can profitably meditate on Gargantua's dictum: "The greatest loss of time that I know is to count the hours. What good comes of it? Nor can there be any greater dotage in the world than for a man to guide and direct his courses by the sound of a bell, and not by his own judgment and discretion." Judgment and discretion, provided their roots are vigorous, burgeon and flourish in solitude.

In the walled town of Saint-Malo the principal hotel was formerly a château, and in one of its rooms a celebrated Breton was born. From the window of that room you can look out across the yellow sands to the shelving rock where the same man lies buried. Most of his long life Chateaubriand had spent far from his native Saint-Malo. He had dallied in Continental capitals, had visited the young United States, had won fame as a colorful prose writer, as a defender of his ancestral faith, as a statesman in days as nearly filled as our own with international perplexities. A picturesque personality, a light of love, a soldier in season and something of a sage, he was a world-arresting figure. In accordance with French custom, the Pantheon should have been his last resting place, but Chateaubriand expressly indicated his desire to lie in death on the shore of the city of his birth, where at high tide the waves submerge the Celtic cross that marks his tomb.

His worldly career had afforded him but few opportunities to indulge his sentiment for solitude. Even when writing the *Génie du christianisme* his manner of life was hardly monastic; but in that book he made it clear that he was— among other and incompatible things—a hermit at heart. Like so many men of today and of all days, Chateaubriand dreamed of withdrawal from the world; like most men, he never actualized the dream. But after life's fitful fever he sleeps well. His storm-lashed sepulcher is a beacon of serenity to all who understand that the Temple of the Spirit looms remote from the bustle of man's work time.

VII THE VALLEY OF SILENCE

"The Wise Rabbi" was the title of a one-act play presented on the old Orpheum circuit. It dealt with the imminent persecution of the Jews in an unnamed principality. The local rabbi, a venerable man, seeking to avert the catastrophe, requested an audience with the prince, a debonair cigarette-smoking sadist who had but to nod his head to bring disaster on the Hebrew population. To a court functionary the rabbi explained, "I should like to have a word with the prince." Notified of the appeal, the prince sardonically curled his lip and ordered the rabbi admitted. "You want a word with me. Well, what is the word? A word is all you shall have— one word. I know what you have come to ask, and if you can put your request into one word it may be that I will grant your plea. But remember, only one word." Then the old rabbi stretched out his arms, pointed to the ghetto and uttered the one word: "Silence!" The prince smiled, and the calamity was averted.

The gift of human speech is an incalculable blessing, and the tongue is mightier than the sword. Through speech man influences his fellow man, offers encouragement, imparts wisdom; through speech he reveals his mind, opens his heart, transmits thoughts and emotions that may flood other souls with inspiration and strength. Through speech the very flesh is made word. The tongue, though a little member, boasteth great things.

But speech has its perils and deafness its compensations. The tongue can be, as Saint James said, a fire, a world of iniquity, an unruly evil, full of deadly poison. Through speech we bless the Father of men, and through speech we curse the children of God. Numerous are the circumstances in daily life and in human relations when we might all profit by the plea of the Wise Rabbi.

Speech rightly used opens a path to the world of the imponderables. Without the spoken and written word we should follow wandering fires and lose ourselves in the quagmires of the spirit. But it is equally true that speech can impede our progress, halt our intellectual and spiritual development. Like Omar Khayyám, we hear much talk about it and about, and came out the same door wherein we went. Mr. Marquand's Jeffrey and Madge were momentarily enriched by standing in the moonlit cathedral—silent. The rule of silence in libraries, in museums, in religious orders is salutary—or would be if it were more sedulously observed. "Beware of much talk," warned a knowing dweller in the Temple of the Spirit, "remain in silence and enjoy thy God."

Unfortunately, speech can be a substitute for both thought and action. The ebullient and loquacious Ulric Brendel in Ibsen's *Rosmersholm* had a horde of world-shattering convictions—"in the rough"; they never got out of the rough. He talked so much that he didn't write anything. Visitors in

Paris used to hear plenty of Brendels endlessly talking in the little restaurants of the Rive Gauche, inglorious Miltons though by no means mute. Those chatterers had projects for novels, poems, dramas, paintings; ideas to quiet the world's unrest and make a new heaven and a new earth—but always in the rough. They might have clarified their thoughts and translated their dreams into constructive action had they but bridled their tongues. There is such a thing as the evaporation of ideas. We know what that popular institution, the mass meeting, amounts to. Talking things over is often tantamount to talking things to death.

Even at its best, talk seldom does more than skim the mind, and the cream is not on the top. Our deepest thoughts are out of reach. Accomplished conversationalists, vitalic lecturers and orators who really say something are able to probe the depths of individual and racial life and to distill the precious liquor of experience and scholarship; priceless is their endowment, and rare. Most of us are pretentious discoverers of the obvious; or, when we have a glimmering of something subtle or recondite, we so maul and torture it in a slather of verbiage that the result is a confusing caricature. The sower of words exacerbates his emotions, talking less to convey ideas than to hit upon ideas; he triturates a topic in the hope—usually vain—of solving a problem or achieving clarity and light by piling words upon words. He is like a man who tries to fill a narrow-necked jug by throwing barrels of water at it.

Much that passes for conversation is flowers without fruit. Pertinently Newman wrote:

Prune thou thy words, the thoughts control
That o'er thee swell and throng;
They will condense within thy soul
And change to purpose strong.

Thought is condensed within the soul as food is digested in the stomach; excessive talk is like cutting a window in the diaphragm to observe the action of the gastric juices. Silence is like cooking a roast or a soufflé; speech like incessantly opening the oven door. Silence is like the photographer's dark room; talking is like turning on the lights to see how the developing fluids work. Cerebration is normally silent. Grover Cleveland, I have somewhere read, once listened to a guest dilate on how to clip cigars. Take your penknife, said the visitor, and cut across the tip of the cigar, but only halfway through; then cut at right angles, removing a wedge and leaving a bowl to hold the moisture. He explained it all elaborately and illustrated his theory by hacking at several cigars. Cleveland listened and watched. Then he took up a cigar, snipped off the end between his teeth and calmly lighted up. He revealed an open mind, a chain of deduction, the weighing of evidence and the translation of thought into action. And he didn't say a word.

Silence may be wise; also, silence may be just plain dumb. "Why, 'tis good to be sad and say nothing," sighed the melancholy Jacques. "Why, then," retorted Rosalind, " 'tis good to be a post." And the same radiant lady voiced Shakespeare's acceptance of the traditional golden mean. To talking versus silence, not less than to gaiety versus glumness, she could bring apt judgment: "Those that are in extremity of either

are abominable fellows and betray themselves to every modern censure worse than drunkards." [1] Silence is a means, not
an end, a means to inner serenity and integrity, a bulwark
against cranks and crackpots, a necessary condition for wor-
shiping in the Temple of the Spirit. Not admirable is the
sour silence of disgruntled victims of *acedia,* the somno-
lent silence of the lazy-minded and empty-headed, the grim
silence of the black-biled introvert, the wary silence of the
writing man who fears his precious ideas might be pilfered
before he can get them into print. Why be so apprehensive
of potential petty larceny?

Few are the men, looking back on their lives, who fail to
mark with a white stone certain hours of genial conversation before the open fire or over the walnuts and the wine.
We can happily recollect dinner parties where wit sparkled
and knowledge glowed, where novel points of view blended
into a friendly symphony of words. On such occasions we
could have said with the ancient Roman, and not merely
on account of the food, "Fate cannot harm me; I have dined
today." Chauncey Depew was an inveterate dinner guest; he
deliberately cultivated after-dinner speaking as a civilized
art and derived from it recreation and enjoyment; he learned
to eat little and speak well. A more cerebral type of man,
Canon William Barry of Leamington, England, also spent
many of his evenings in dining rooms and drawing rooms, and
he assures us in his autobiography that he derived immense
intellectual profit from the practice. Man is a social being
and he thrives on the give and take of table talk.

[1] *As You Like It,* IV, 1.

111

Nevertheless it must be admitted that, in numerous instances, to accept dinner invitations is to waste time, to face boredom and to suffer dissipation of mind. It all depends, of course, on where you go and whom you meet; and blessed are you if you enter an atmosphere akin to those seventeenth-century Paris salons where abbés and atheists, politicos and poets could foregather in urbane amity. Molière, to be sure, had his fun with the bluestockings in *Les Précieuses Ridicules,* and vastly amused the illiterate, boar-hunting, hard-drinking husbands of the women who cultivated good taste and refined manners. It was those same women, typified in Madame de Rambouillet, who established standards in entertainment and conversation, standards which have made France a nation of courteous people who enjoy freshness of thought, cleverness in conversation and the savor of words on the tongue. A catalytic hostess is a gift from heaven, but heaven is sparing of such gifts. Instead, there is all too often the consciously tactful and masterful woman who strains herself to "keep things going well," which means keeping everybody talking at the same time. She dreads a lull more than a shattered aspic. To Whistler a lull was a relief: "You know, I enjoy these lucid intervals."

How Mr. Smith lost his faith is no more a fit table topic than how Mrs. Smith lost her vermiform appendix. Have we not body clinics and soul clinics for self-indulgence in expatiating on heartburn and heresy, scrofula and satyriasis? "Of course, if you understand right away what a painting is all about, it can't be great art, can it?" "I feel so much when I hear a symphony, but I don't know what it means, if you know what I mean." "I didn't see a sanitary sewer system in Costa Rica, but then you have to make allowances for those backward peoples." "Things must be a mess in Germany now, but you can't believe everything you read in the newspapers." How disappointing to expect a feast of reason and a flow of soul, and get a salad of banalities with solecism dressing.

Satan overlooked one expedient when he tempted the patient Job. The holy man of Uz never had to listen to a lady more plump than pleasing contribute to universal knowledge by pontificating, "Now, *my* idea of religion is simply *this* . . ." Herbert Spencer knew what to do in such cases. He carried a pair of earmuffs—those benighted Victorians had no gas masks—and he calmly put them on when inane talk drove him into the valley of silence:

> Said the Young Old Man to the Old Young Man—
> *I'm a trifle hard of hearing.*

Earmuffs would be a convenience in smoking compartments, hotel lobbies and airport waiting rooms where strangers insist on asking personal questions and confiding episodes, not always honorable and never interesting, in their private lives. Even the Catholic Church discourages the public confession of sins, save in general formulas which allow scant play for complacency in moral aberrations and doctrinal divagations. It is humble—and whispered—confession that is reputedly good for the soul.

It is probable that some people have grown disgusted with music and art, philosophy and religion, because they have had to listen to so much mediocre and uninspired talk on those important subjects. "It is a great pity," wrote John Keats, "that people should by associating themselves with the finest things, spoil them. . . . Hunt does one harm by making fine things petty and beautiful things hateful. Through him I am indifferent to Mozart, I care not for white busts—and many a glorious thing when associated with him becomes a nothing."

As a fighting editor and as an exponent of what the reviewers dubbed the Cockney School of Poetry, Leigh Hunt exerted a far from negligible influence on the life and thought of his day, but it would seem that he did altogether too much talking. "If he has a fault," wrote Hazlitt, "it is that he does not listen as well as he speaks, is impatient of interruption, and is fond of being looked up to, without considering by whom." The same gentle censure might be tossed at many a preacher and teacher—in and out of office hours—and at swarms of facile discoursers on music, art and literature. The assiduous and ecstatic convert-maker—to Yoga or eugenics, Rachmaninoff or righteousness—often stimulates perverse and irrational opposition in his browbeaten hearers. After all, comparatively few of us are divinely commissioned to preach the gospel to every creature.

Silence and solitude are traditionally linked, for silence is a prelude to solitude, and solitude is facilitated by absence of talk. The silence of a strong, sensitive, thinking man has majesty and charm. The Temple of the Spirit can be built nowhere but in the silent places; it is the Tower of Babel that symbolizes a confusion of tongues. Silence conduces to a steady and steadying outlook on life and history, makes the art of reflection possible and contributes to an objective scrutiny of ideas, opinions and plans. In silence we learn to know ourselves, to analyze our motives and our emotions. However imperious, the urgings of pride and lust, avarice and ambition, lose much of their power when investigated in the cold light of silence. And only in silence may we listen to the music of the spheres.

To become what Dr. Harry Emerson Fosdick calls a real person, to attain to a high degree of psychological integration, is impossible without possessing interior peace; and peace is impossible without the practice of silence. Incessant chatter disrupts and corrupts personality, brings about that wasteful diffusion of mind and spirit known as the schizophrenic condition—a horrible word and a horrible state. One indication of an unbalanced personality is the tendency to talk overmuch and to write lengthy letters on the slightest pretext. The words wholeness, health and holiness all come from the same root, and the human qualities they stand for are basically one. If the world has forgotten that, if the schizophrenic mentality has chopped religion, philosophy and the arts off the tree of life and denied their essential unity, it is to a considerable extent due to the neglect of the virtue of silence. For silence is virtue and *virtus,* grace and manly strength.

Silence offers a germinating period to the soul. It allows our hidden energies, more potent than we realize, to renew their vigor, to recharge our batteries and so to make our lives and our works successful and significant. The second wind of the mind, as explained by William James in "The Energies of Man," rarely becomes a reality in an atmosphere of talk; usually it attains its maximum during or soon after a session of silent thought.

Father Frederick Faber observed in one of his essays that priests who habitually give missions, preaching several times a day and moving from city to city every week or two, are seldom deeply spiritual men. They meet too many people and they talk too much. That fact is recognized in religious congregations devoted largely to mission activities. The missioners are allowed occasional periods to refresh their spirits in solitude and silence. A similar need is felt by experienced and thoughtful men who tour the country giving lectures; they stay at hotels rather than in the homes of friends, and they are chary about accepting invitations to luncheons and dinners. They are not antisocial, they are wise; for they have learned they must balance one hour of lecturing with two or more hours of silence. They could, of course, go on for a while carried by the momentum of habit and prestige; but if they are, as they ought to be, their own best critics, they soon detect the folly of burning their candle at both ends. Without seasons of thoughtful silence they find staleness and superficiality marring even their most conscientiously prepared discourses. Richard Henry Stoddard, one of the most capable and popular lecturers ever heard in the United States, spent nearly half of every year in Europe, assembling his material and ruminating on it; while still a young man he withdrew from lecturing and settled down with his books and his memories in a Tyrolese town.

The musician, the painter, the writer may be the life of the party in nightclub or at clambake, letting off steam, spouting sparkling nonsense, clinking glasses, paying extravagant compliments and having a rattling good time. With Horace, they believe in playing the fool in proper season. But not always do they kick antic heels and clash cymbals in Naxos. They do their serious work in complete solitude and rigorous silence. They are like the actress, cast for the lead in *A Doll's House*, who informed her café society friends, "I'm going out into the woods for a few weeks to find my Nora." Then, there was the artist who had a flagpole on the lawn of his suburban home. If the flag flew, visitors were welcome; if not, they honored him by keeping away. One of his neighbors, a successful writer and a thoroughly married man, made sure of spells of silence by climbing to his attic workshop, pulling the brass ladder up after him and slamming down the trapdoor. So he wrote and raved in unbroken silence while downstairs his little children romped or his wife entertained at bridge and tea.

For him who would dwell in the Temple of the Spirit noise and talk make an unfavorable environment. In the face of an unfavorable environment there are only three things to do: we can submit to it, and lose our souls; we can flee to the woods and maybe find our Nora; we can create in the midst of tumult an oasis of peace. Such an oasis was Carlyle's house in Chelsea, with its soundproof room shutting out the clatter of drays and the cries of hawkers and admitting only the muted rumble of the unresting metropolis. There Carlyle and Tennyson—"such company over a pipe!"—indulged in "speculation free and plenteous," too friendly to mind long spaces of silence. Such was the self-imposed rule of John Middleton Murry and his wife Katherine Mansfield, living in a French town. They read and wrote in a tiny room, penalizing each other for every breach of silence until the clock announced the end of the working period.

One compensation for living in London is the presence of unsuspected pools of silence off Fleet Street and High Holborn—Ely Place, for instance, and Wine Office Court, when shrill-voiced American tourists are not descending on the Cheshire Cheese. Footfalls actually echo on the flags. Shops and dwellings suggest a monastery of the strict observance. A peep in at a window reveals a clerk who looks like Charles Lamb bent over a ponderous ledger, a pottery worker shaping his wares, a watchman straight out of Dickens cuddling a seasoned pipe. In such spots Richardson wrote *Clarissa*, and Goldsmith *She Stoops to Conquer*, and the homesick young Yeats heard "lake water lapping with low sounds by the shore."

In a Roman church stands a statue of Saint Bruno, the man who founded the Carthusians and inculcated in his rule the strict practice of silence. It is an admirably executed piece of sculpture, though somehow not widely known, and it has elicited admiration from discerning critics. One of them, a Frenchman, gazed at it long and searchingly. Then he said: "That statue would speak, did not the Carthusian rule impose perpetual silence."

Manifestly, perpetual silence is not a vocation that most mortals could gracefully accept, and the heroicity of its extreme may not even seem admirable; yet the suave diplomat —suavity once was a diplomatic virtue—the wily politician, the frenzied financier and the man who solicits insurance could each and all meditate with profit on the advantages of an approximation, however remote, to good Saint Bruno's idea. They all talk too much, trip over their tongues, employ the faculty of speech to conceal the absence of thought. The Mavericks have a word for it: gobbledygook.

In one of those digressions, often more meaty than the narratives in which they occur, Thackeray said that when good fellows get together, in their series of libations there comes a phenomenon which might be designated the magic glass. Before that climactic moment a man is taciturn and ill at ease; when it is passed he is sillily sentimental and perhaps offensively truculent. The *summum bonum* of practical sagacity is to drink up to the magic glass, and then stop.

Applied to conviviality, I suspect, the magic-glass formula is a counsel of perfection that puts a severe strain on the tensile strength of human self-control; but it can be and ought to be a guiding principle in the use of the tongue. How many speakers know when to stop? Polonius was no fool when he protested against the player's fustian speech, "This is too long." We have all known a fellow feeling with Polonius while we squirmed in a church pew or the visitors' gallery of the august United States Senate. We have envied the courage of Polonius while we listlessly listened to a festive monologist who had palpably passed beyond his magic glass. And there are times when, if we cultivate the ascetic art of listening to ourselves, we shall be certain that Polonius was

119

a constructive critic. He gabbled interminably himself, of course, but that is another story.

Three minutes of silence. At public meetings, at a football game, in the course of a cemetery pilgrimage, the tribute of respect is paid to a man, a country, an ideal. Everybody bows his head—sometimes with a perceptible list to starboard—and during three minutes nobody utters a word. A silence of three minutes is about all the group mentality can stand, but the individual, for the good of his digestion and his soul, might carry the idea a little further. Why not a daily golden hour of silence? Disconnect the telephone, turn off the radio, be firm with your secretary or your cook, and during one solid hour keep your mouth shut. You need not do it in a mental and emotional vacuum. You can read, preferably something really worth reading. You can think, preferably with pencil in hand. You can bring back forgotten joys and vanished faces and youth beyond recall. You can meditate on the last discourse of Socrates, the opening of the Fourth Gospel, "The Chambered Nautilus." You can revive the memory of Rimski-Korsakoff's Easter medley heard in the Berkshires and a Massenet program rendered by an international orchestra in the Piazza of San Marco. You can hold the mind to one field of thought, or you can run the gamut of purifying emotions. You can even—though it is advisable to be discreet in this—think about yourself. Nothing greatly matters so long as your golden hour of silence has a beginning, a middle and an end. You don't require Carlyle's soundproof room, for you have fashioned for the moment a room of your own. You don't need to follow Saint Bruno into the

Valley of Chartreuse, for you have found your own Valley of Silence.

The imponderables would mean more and accomplish more in the days and ways of men if we cherished them more and argued about them less. If so many well-meaning persons egregiously misunderstand the nature, the functions and the spirit of religion, it is largely because of the vocal activities of militant controversialists, sectarian politicians and presumptuous amateur theologians who lack experience, spiritual insight and historical perspective. It is in the silence that God speaks to us and we to Him—the silence of the pathless woods and the desert sands, the silence of the humble spirit and the understanding heart. In silence the influences of eternity impregnate the soul, and in silence they overflow into our daily lives.

To talk overmuch about the arts is to distort and vulgarize them. Music, painting, sculpture, poetry speak their own language, and to try to translate their elusive essence into commonplace words is like trying to convey the majesty of the deep-voiced ocean in terms of meteorology. Goethe and Browning were neither absurd nor inconsistent when they admitted inability to tell what some of their writings meant; the second part of *Faust* and the allegedly obscure passages in *The Ring and the Book* are unintelligible only to the commonplace and literal-minded reader. Discussion of the arts seldom brings light and understanding. The arts transcend argument and conventional scholarship; like moonlight and mother love, they bestow benefits that baffle analysis. Nobody can describe the charm of Bourgereau's *Fifferero* or the

121

Finlandia of Sibelius; but those masterpieces do something for us, something not merely emotional, something beyond and above prettiness and ear-tickling. The arts must be enjoyed in silent ecstasy:

> And kneeling, breathless, in the holy place
> We know immortal beauty face to face.

The study of philosophy involves talk, sometimes good talk, and the masters of thought have often utilized the spoken word; but neither masters nor pupils are talking all the time. The thinkers who congregated in the Painted Porch and the young men who clustered about Socrates were good listeners and they had opportunities to think in silence. Abélard, Albert the Great and Duns Scotus knew the solace and inspiration of monastic seclusion and in its great silence their thoughts condensed within their souls. Necessary yet insidiously dangerous is the philosopher's gift of tongues. It can stimulate intellectual auto-intoxication and foster pettiness, cocksureness and scholarly spleen. I like to believe that it was a genial and reverent philosopher who elaborated an edifying legend commemorating another man of thought. Saint Thomas Aquinas, good portly man, was puffing down a priory corridor some minutes after the bell had rung for office in the chapel. From her pedestal the Blessed Virgin admonished him: "Brother Thomas, you are late." Respectfully the philosopher-monk put his finger to his lips, bowed reverently and replied: "Mother Mary, you are breaking silence."

VIII RADIANT ISLES

IMMERSED in the torrent of war books that came to us during recent years, readers eager for fine and thoughtful works of fiction may have missed *Lost Island,* by Mr. James Norman Hall. Even those who have acclaimed him as co-author of *Mutiny on the Bounty, The Hurricane* and *Botany Bay* may have missed knowing Mr. Hall as a gentle philosopher and an appreciator of the imponderables—for in *Lost Island* that is what he is. He tells of a tiny island in the Pacific Ocean where the soft-eyed natives and a handful of assorted white men lead hidden, happy lives. The climate is genial, the scenery impressive, the moral atmosphere salubrious. Farmers and fishermen work leisurely, two refugees from war-racked Europe interpret Mozart's sonatas on moonlit nights, the aged priest rejoices in the church he has built and the glowing gardens beside the sacred walls. Of a sudden, under the grim imperative of war, the United States Navy takes over the little island. White-clad sailors unload drums of gasoline, bulldozers tear up the soil and raucous voices day and night shatter the silence of the village street. The padre's garden and the church itself are destroyed to make room for gun emplacements, and the decency and simplicity of the inhabitants dissolve before the onset of progress and civilization. The radiant isle becomes a casualty of war.

That lost island is a symbol of the tragedy which takes place, often imperceptibly, in many human lives. Man *is* a ruminating animal, and without thought, reflection, contemplation, his soul is empty and his works are vain. His nature craves, among other and obvious things, a silent sanctuary, a radiant isle, a time and place for meditation. Periodically he must withdraw from work and play to renew his inner youth, to recharge his spiritual batteries, to clarify his vision and fortify his soul. He must look into himself in the light of eternal values, correct the deflections of his personal compass, restore his sense of proportion, plan his life in accordance with first things and last things. The need for reflection is recognized by everyone, save possibly the extreme extrovert. But to recognize the need is not necessarily to make time and place for filling the need. The world presses in upon us, commandeers our every hour, drains our last trickle of energy. Business and politics, war and diplomacy, amusement and society invade our privacy as ruthlessly as the navy imposed itself on Mr. Hall's island. "With desolation is all the land made desolate because there is no man that considereth in his heart."

On a day in September, 1944, an overseas dispatch announced: "An island of light emerged from the European sea of darkness last night when little Switzerland came out of its four-year-long total blackout." Suffering from inadvertent bombings by Allied planes, the Swiss decided to mark their boundaries with illuminations. The news was significant in more ways than one. Through more than six centuries Switzerland has been indeed an island of light and peace in the heart of a continent repeatedly ravaged by international strife. The Swiss, like all of us, have troubles of their own, and the earlier decades of their history were scarred with conflict; they fought against their neighbors and they fought among themselves. But through experience and common sense they learned to win the respect of other nations and to settle their own racial and religious disputes. Their national self-interest led, not to aggression and imperialism, but to self-contained solidarity and independence.

The turning on of the lights in Switzerland as the European war drew to a close might well be accepted as an allegory. Every man who lives deeply and richly cannot win to inner serenity and steadiness of vision without turning on the lights. Around him hangs the darkness of suspicion and strife, of ignorance and malice, of thoughtlessness and moral chaos; he can save his soul only by dwelling on the radiant isle of constructive meditation, allowing his spirit to be guided and invigorated by the fruitage which only the imponderables can yield.

Meditation means more than thinking things out. It is cognitive, but not exclusively so. It involves more than an inductive synthesis or a rigidly logical deduction. It takes in the whole man. It utilizes emotion and it normally tends to the exercise of volition. It is flexibly systematic, without being chained to any rigid method. A man meditates when, in the widest meaning of the terms, he goes into his chamber and shuts the door and prays to his Father in secret. Narrowly considered, it may not be a religious practice, for the praying is not always conscious prayer; but inevitably it involves a temporary withdrawal from the material world and an immersion in what Goethe called the enduring relations of life.

The traditional wisdom of thinkers in the East and in the West has stressed the necessity of meditation and has formulated detailed rules for securing facility in the exercise of it. Such rules are to be accepted with merited respect and employed with judicious discernment. Method was made for man, not man for method. In itself a method is neither good nor bad. It is good, as Dr. Wolfgang Kohler says, "if it is properly adapted to the essential aspects of my problems and my material." [1] It is bad when it cramps intellectual and emotional freedom, when its aims are too vague or too narrowly practical; when, after honest effort, we find it to be ill-suited to our individual nature and needs. And even a method of meditation once fruitful and effective can be outgrown; the fumbling neophyte and the mature thinker each requires a method of his own. The tyro wants to learn how to meditate, how to overcome the difficulties inherent in the art; the veteran wants to preserve his knowledge—of literature or art or religion—from dry rot and shrinkage, to keep it fresh and aerated, to incorporate it into the texture of his daily life; above all, to expand and deepen those intimations of eternity that penetrate like spears of sunlight the umbrageous limitations of time. No one method can serve those different ends.

[1] *Gestalt Psychology*, p. 38.

Meditation degenerates into vapid daydreaming if devoid of some sort of skeletal structure, just as unplanned writing results in a maze or a mush of impressions. We should be rationally methodical without becoming undiscriminating methodists. The basic structure of every form of art, including the art of meditation, was formulated with subtle simplicity by Aristotle: It should have a beginning, a middle and an end. A drama—any drama, ancient or modern, that is a drama at all—rises to its climax and descends to its conclusion. The structure of it follows a triangular pattern, though the triangle is not always equilateral; the climax or high place may occur midway between beginning and end, or it may come shortly before the conclusion.

So, in meditating, we start somewhere, we go somewhere else, and thence we arrive at a cognate consequence. Some authorities recommend that the beginning be an act of intellect, the middle an act of emotion and the conclusion an act of will. I gravely doubt that such regimentation of the mind is either necessary or desirable. Man is seldom a purely thinking animal, his emotional moments are rarely untouched by some degree of cognition, and his thinking and his feeling—especially the latter—generate acts of the will. Thus, if I think about an impoverished family across the railroad tracks, I simultaneously experience feelings of sympathy, grief, perhaps indignation, and my conative discharge will be, "I'll send them a check," or "Something should be done about it," or "There ought to be a law."

The conative or volitional element in meditation takes the form of some kind of resolution. We are told that every reso-

127

lution should be (1) particular, (2) present and (3) efficacious; that is, it should (1) be specific, get down to cases; it should (2) pertain to our conduct in the immediate future; and it should (3) be buttressed with clearly envisaged means of putting it into effect and with self-imposed sanctions or penalties in case of failure to keep the resolution. That threefold safeguard of conative action can be helpful, especially for the beginner whose volitional fervor may easily dissipate itself in diffused determination to "do better after this" or "turn over a new leaf." Yet meditation may be rich and profitable without it. The late Bishop Hedley once pointed out that immense value inheres in a general resolution, that a far-off goal, even cloudily envisaged, can be a potent inspiration. If a man decides to walk from Newark to Pompton Lakes, his mind and his feet are set in the right direction, even though he does not specifically resolve, "At one o'clock I will be in East Orange and an hour later I will cross the Watchung Range." In "The Gospel of Relaxation" William James suggests that resolutions excessively detailed and specific may impede rather than aid progress. The experts mean well and many of them know whereof they speak, but their prescriptions, sedulously and literally followed, may lead only to confusion and anxiety.

Even as the most ethereal poet must have something to write about, so the man who meditates must have material of some sort to ruminate upon. Much of that material is supplied by books. Many persons cannot meditate because they do too little reading, and the remedy for their insufficiency of ideas is obvious. But other persons, though their plight may seem paradoxical, fail to meditate because they read too much. Their passion for fact can easily dull their perception of truth. According to temperament and training, they may hold the facts higgledy-piggledy like the odds and ends in an untidy junk shop, or—and in this case they have reason to be a little complacent—they may keep the fruitage of their reading in a memory as compact and accessible as a cross-indexed filing system; but in either case it can happen that the very abundance of the material for thought impedes the process of thinking. Like Henry Adams' students at Harvard, they may dig up data like rabbits, but they are impotent to sift and winnow the contents of their minds.

Wordsworth's description of poetry, powerful emotion recollected in tranquillity, has considerable bearing on all forms of meditation. We recall the literature and philosophy we have read, the pictures we have seen, the cities we have visited, the mountains we have scaled, the words and the faces of men and women esteemed and loved. Numerous details slip out of consciousness, but what remains is probably what we most acutely need; at least, it is most in consonance with our tastes and interests and the structure of our personality. An all-retaining memory is as fatal as the Midas touch. The Bourbons never learned anything *because* they never forgot anything. When the mind reflects, turning back on its contents in the light of new experience, it is meditating; but the process of meditation, as Plutarch says in the introduction to his life of Pericles, is based on selection, and selection necessarily implies rejection. Both the junk-shop mind and the filing-system mind do not know how to select

129

and reject, and to them meditation is difficult and often impossible.

As with method, so with time and place for meditation; it is hazardous to lay down hard and fast rules. In religious orders, where meditation or mental prayer is a daily obligation, the place is the chapel and the time early morning. That prescription has manifest advantages—freshness of mind, absence of external distractions, a suitable environment. But there are disadvantages too. Does everybody feel mentally vigorous in the morning's dim light? A church or chapel, an art gallery or museum, looks at first like an ideal place for meditation; but in some instances, and for various reasons, it proves to be a compelling place for slumber.

It is possible to meditate anywhere at any time—canoeing in the evening, hiking at the break of dawn, pruning a tree in midafternoon. The novelist Meredith Nicholson claimed he did his best thinking while shaving; and I recall an eminent philosopher whose intellectual processes functioned most felicitously when, as he put it, "I assume a horizontal posture." It was in a horizontal posture, legend says, that Walter Pater sometimes delivered his lectures at Oxford. Yet taking one's meditation lying down is not to be enthusiastically recommended. Those earnest gentlemen like Mr. Bernard Shaw who awaken early and toss and think, confess that they usually dwell on troubles and difficulties which darkness magnifies rather than dissipates.

Erect or recumbent, it is not advisable to make the period of meditation a time for tortuous review of our temporal and spiritual problems. Meditation should not be egocentric and introspective, an orgy of narcissism. Saint Bernard, certainly no ivory-tower monk, at the beginning of his meditation deliberately banished his duties, responsibilities and irritations: "I shall meet you again when I leave the chapel." Vitalizing meditation is not the prolonged contemplation of our navel, much less picking at mental scabs and squeezing spiritual pimples. Soul expansion does not come that way. Rather, all meditation should approximate to Dryden's definition of meditation on history: "The most pleasant school of wisdom . . . a perspective-glass carrying your soul to a vast distance, and taking in the farthest objects of antiquity." [2]

The one absolute essential for meditation is concern with the imponderables. We meditate, not to get into ourselves, but to get out of ourselves. No value inheres in the kind of meditating that parallels the amateur photographer showing "me and the Grand Canal," "me on a donkey in Cairo," "me against the white cliffs of Dover." The most exalted states of prayer are not prayers of petition but of union with God and immersion in God; and the most enriching way to read poetry is to lose oneself in the poem. Great music blows into us, and we are conscious of the music rather than of ourselves. A man may profitably sit for an hour before a noble picture, but not if all the while or much of the while he is dissecting his reactions to the painting. Those knowing patrons of the drama who enjoy seeing innumerable productions of *Hamlet* are adepts in meditation, for when they see Mr. Maurice Evans they recall Mr. John Gielgud and Mr. Walter Hampden, E. H. Sothern and Forbes-Robertson; and

[2] Preface to *Plutarch's Lives* (Dublin, 1769), p. xliv.

all the time their individual lives are but wires whereon are strung the beads of memories and impressions. As for philosophy, we know that lack of impersonality clouds issues and blinds the eyes of the mind: "There ain't no sich animal" if the animal fails to conform to the prejudices and preconceptions of my particular philosophic tribe.

But, somebody might object, if you don't think about yourself when meditating, what good does it do you? The question is answered by another: If you don't think about saliva and gastric juices when eating your dinner, what good does it do you? In both instances the benefits are secured without our taking thought of ourselves. The man much traveled in the realms of gold, the man of disciplined character and mature mind and wide acquaintance with the imponderables, does surprisingly little thinking about himself—he has more important things on his mind. He can speak correctly without thinking about grammar, he is urbane and gracious without resolving to be nice to people, and his casual comments may reveal a vast knowledge of art and music, literature and philosophy, without his making the slightest effort to display his inner wealth. His air of ease and gentility is not a pose, an affectation, a studied means of impressing other men; it is the spontaneous and unconscious flowering of life within the Temple of the Spirit.

The great day comes when a man begins to get himself off his hands. He has lived, let us say, in a mind like a room surrounded by mirrors. Every way he turned he saw himself. Now, however, some of the mirrors change to windows. He can see through them to objective outlooks that challenge his interests.

He begins to get out of himself—no longer the prisoner of self-reflections but a free man in a world where persons, causes, truths and values exist, worthful for their own sakes. Thus to pass from a mirror mind to a mind with windows is an essential element in the development of real personality. Without that experience no one ever achieves a meaningful life.[3]

Meditation is known by its fruits. The human sponge, who, as Coleridge says, absorbs material, retains it unchanged and when squeezed yields it only a little dirtier, might as well not meditate at all. The same is true of the strain-bag mentality which retains only the dregs of reading and experience; to it meditation is the dispiriting contemplation of human depravity, of greed and vanity, stupidity and spite and scandals in high places. Why can we not be as fastidious about what we put into our mind as about what we put into our stomach? Unwise, to say the least, is the meditation which induces despondency, cynicism, spiritual paralysis, lack of charity and loss of faith. It is a poor philosophy which transmutes a radiant isle into a lost island.

He who would learn the art of meditation might reflect on Ariel's song in *The Tempest:*

> Full fathom five thy father lies;
> Of his bones are coral made;
> Those are pearls that were his eyes:
> Nothing of him that doth fade
> But doth suffer a sea-change
> Into something rich and strange.

[3] Harry Emerson Fosdick: *On Being a Real Person,* p. 84. © 1943. Published by Harper & Brothers.

The sea-changes of the spirit vitalize and glorify the material absorbed. The result is something rich, that is, something valuable and precious; and it is something strange, that is, something novel in form, possessing the charm and challenge of variety. Meditation makes all things new. The material it works on it transforms and re-creates. Sponges and strain-bags need the reminder given by Epictetus: "Sheep do not hastily throw up the grass, to show the shepherds how much they have eaten; but inwardly digesting their food, they produce it outwardly in wool and milk."

We may measure our progress in the art of meditating by noting the extent to which we thus transform the books we read, the music we hear and the very lives we live. After the first fervor of the beginner wears off there is a stage of weariness, barrenness, spiritual aridity, due in large degree to our inability to get out of ourselves, to minimize the demands of our narrow personal interests. This dark night of the soul, as Saint John of the Cross called it, endures indefinitely; some men never get out of it at all, and to them meditating is a trial and a chore which yields no satisfaction other than the consciousness of having tried to do something worth doing. But normally there comes a time—and here all authorities are in accord—when the human spirit experiences a sense of ease and release. Then we grasp the meaning of Cardinal Newman's motto, *Ex umbris et imaginibus in veritatem,* we pass from shadows and symbols into the realm of ultimate beauty and truth. We lose track of time, we grow indifferent to posture and place. The body and its cravings, the surface mind and its preoccupations seem remote and unimportant.

We are in a sense depersonalized and sublimated and come to know what eye hath not seen nor ear heard nor the heart of man conceived. We dwell in the Temple of the Spirit.

In the art of meditation all the imponderables work together unto good. Visitors to Siena during the *palio* recall that in the great black and white marble duomo the wooden floor coverings are taken up and the magnificent pavement carvings are laid bare, carvings depicting Biblical episodes and historical events, mythological fancies and legends of the saints, traditional incentives to virtuous living and those seven ages of man which Shakespeare immortalized in *As You Like It.* Poised above those pavement sermons in stone, the exquisitely wrought marble pulpit seems superfluous. Midway down the nave, on the gospel side, a massive door offers access to a vaulted room that is a library and a picture gallery combined. Dedicated to the memory of the humanist Aeneas Sylvius, later Pope Pius II, that unique chapel of the human spirit draws no censorious distinction between religion and art, past and present, sacred and profane. The responsive visitor finds naught incongruous in turning the illuminated pages of a Renaissance fable while the music of the *Gloria* drifts in from the unseen sanctuary. The cathedral of Siena might well serve as an archetype for the Temple of the Spirit.

The isles of contemplation offer what many men desire and all men need—a season of isolation from the clamorous urgencies of mundane life, from the impertinences and abrasions of bread-winning and vote-getting and those unrests and worries which are about the only contribution helplessly benevolent mortals bring to the healing of the nations. The radiant isles supply an environment wherein we may recognize and in some measure rectify "our general human habit of appraising everything from irrelevant standpoints." [4] The habit of reflection, projected into practical action, may help to save us from the drabness of daily life so accurately indicated by Mr. Cabell:

> Pure reason—I mean as pure as human reason assays—reveals out of hand that the main course of daily living is part boredom, part active discomfort and fret, and, for the not inconsiderable rest, a blundering adherence to some standard derived from this or that hearsay.[5]

The bored, like the bores, are always with us; but neither of them flock to the radiant isles. Everywhere the sons of Adam succumb to active discomfort, but only when they are engrossed in material interests, and that same debasing addiction robs them of tranquillity of soul. Meditation can, and normally does, bring forgetfulness of malaise; and if in some instances it blows up brainstorms it as often allays the tempests of the spirit. While some men need to be shaken up, other men need to be shaken down. As for standards derived from hearsays, no place is better than the radiant isles for scrutinizing and evaluating the credentials of the hearsayers and the soothsayers and for giving happy allegiance to those pregnant principles concerning which the great minds of the

[4] James Branch Cabell: *Beyond Life*, p. 86. © 1919, 1927, 1946 by the author.

[5] James Branch Cabell: *Straws and Prayer-Books*, p. 27. ©1924, 1930 by the author. Published by Robert McBride & Co.

race are consolingly unanimous. Isolated indeed those isles of reflection may be, but not remote from essential reality, for their rocky cliffs and sheltered beaches are washed by the universal sea.

IX SNOW-BRIGHT MOUNTAINS

THE Temple of the Spirit will never be crowded with worshipers, for the Temple of the Spirit is the dwelling place of peace. As it is and as it has been, the world is a field of strife. Even when the war drums throb no longer and the battle flags are furled, the nations seethe with unrest and sus-picion, employing the resources of science to devise more deadly weapons for the next fratricidal conflict. Larger and larger standing armies, more and more treasure poured out for munitions and armament, intensive training of young men in the arts of human slaughter are judged necessary to secure national solidarity and international respect.

Dogs, as the estimable Isaac Watts pointed out in his *Divine and Moral Songs for Children,* may delight to bark and bite, and bears and lions to growl and fight, but at least they do not organize themselves into armies to prey upon their own species. The beasts are not intelligent enough for that! War and the war spirit is the exclusive accomplishment of man—Idiots' Delight, as Mr. Robert Sherwood has aptly characterized it, a futile and irrational activity not unfairly satirized by Karel Capek in *The Insect Play.* Gentlemen may cry peace, peace, but there is no peace. Tennyson's noble vision of the parliament of man and the federation of the world would be a dusty, sweaty arena of spite and greed, conflicting interests and ambitions.

Nor does peace prevail within the nation and the smaller political groups. Neither totalitarianism nor democracy functions without violence, recrimination, intemperate controversy and prostitution of decency and truth. Party wars with party, class with class. It is a commonplace that any man who aspires to public office must be a fighter, and sufficiently thick-skinned to withstand scurrilous attacks on his character and motives. A modern equivalent of Rome's gladiatorial shows is the weekly meeting of the local board of supervisors where public servants perpetuate internecine feuds or gang up on city manager or mayor. At the circus—this is a natural transition—the daring young man on the flying trapeze would often like to wring the neck of the equally daring young woman whom he catches in midair twice daily; and he graphically symbolizes the state of mind of other sleek and competent performers—the big executive, the academic dean, the twentieth-century Bishop Blougram, the ink-squirting editor and the mannish lady president of some society for the preservation of peace. Behind the scenes of every charity football game, civic pageant, grand opera season and art exhibit hangs a steamy stench of animosities, antipathies, double-crossing and character assassination reminiscent of Browning's "Soliloquy of the Spanish Cloister." To the cleared and polished desk of the company director clings the fetid odor of interminable wranglings, browbeatings and epithet-hurling good-will sessions. Maybe it is news

140

when a man bites a dog; it certainly isn't news—even in Washington—when one man bites another.

Moralists, many of them celibates, descant on the happiness of family life, on the harmonious relations of man, wife and child. Such eulogies are often justified, for many a family is indeed an abode of peace; but, alas, not all families. We do not have to turn to the sordid and vulgar records of the divorce courts to discover that marriage and parenthood do not automatically bring the peace that passeth understanding. Family life, like community life, has its tensions and cross-purposes and animosities, its upsurges of violence and its seasons of sullen disharmony. "There's no place like home," George Ade once wrote, "and some men are glad of it." Man and wife can grow together, but just as readily they can grow apart. Certain psychologists even go so far as to see in married life less a fusion of personalities than a conflict of the sexes. And conflict is the word for the relations between many children and parents, conflict exacerbated by ignorance, tyranny, selfishness, lack of discipline and absence of ideals. Sometimes what passes for peace is the armed neutrality of basic antagonisms, that vipers' tangle so relentlessly depicted by François Mauriac.

If we fall short of peace in the world, in the nation, in the community and in the family itself, if we are persuaded that conflict is normal and natural, even inevitable and desirable, it is largely because the priceless benison of peace has not glorified the individual soul. We lay the blame for strife on other nations, other classes, other persons, but the primal source of conflict is in the deep heart's core. Put a man on a remote uninhabited island, and his spirit can be a battleground of swirling impulses and darkling desires. The flesh warreth against the spirit and the spirit against the flesh.

"Is it weakness of intellect, birdie," I cried,
"Or a rather tough worm in your little inside?"

Probably both. Man's life on earth has been called a perpetual warfare, and numerous reputable and reverend writers have designated man's aspirations after higher things as the spiritual conflict. Even in the field of the imponderables we have commended the fighting spirit. "I was ever a fighter," boasts the poet; "I have fought the good fight," boasts the saint. Nor did Landor approximate to the spirit of peace—the fact is, he told a whopping lie—when he wrote, "I strove with none, for none was worth my strife." Yes, the vulture of dissension tears the heart of man; he can find peace nowhere but in the Temple of the Spirit.

Like love, like understanding, peace on earth can come only when individual men establish it within their own souls. It is not brought about through international alliances, trade pacts and tariffs high or low, or through the hypocritical suavities of power diplomacy. Of what use is it, as Ruskin said, for men to put their heads together unless first they put their hearts together? Only more contention comes from the conference table where the conferees are devoid of interior peace. Until each of them settles his own inner conflicts all of them are helpless to win peace for groups. The objectives and methods of mass production, admirable and effective in turning out tractors and tommy guns, are useless when employed to quell quarrels and dissipate dissensions. Seek the roots of disastrous conflicts between nations and classes and sects, and invariably you find a man, often gifted and resourceful, who has failed to master his own inner turmoil—a neurotic, perhaps, or an epileptic, a slave of sensuality or of pride—who diffuses the bitterness and desperation of his tortured soul among masses and classes and vitiates the clean air with the psychic poisons of suspicion and hatred and vindictiveness. We allow such men to rise, we retain them in places of influence, and then we wonder why rational human beings cannot live together in amity. Men are at war with one another because each man is at war with himself. "That which cometh out of the man, that defileth the man"—and the world which man has made.

Wherefore has it been written, "The mountains shall bring peace." For the mountains of our human history are the master accomplishments of master minds; not the master minds that have ruled nations and waged wars and enslaved their fellows by force or by craft, but the spiritual leaders, the prophets, the teachers, the fosterers, the inspirers, the seers—Isaiah, John of the Fourth Gospel, Plato, Thomas à Kempis, Phidias, Velasquez, Virgil, Cicero, Bach, Beethoven, Dante, Shakespeare and all the others who, in philosophy and poetry, in art and religion, have in one way or another captured and transmitted the breath and finer spirit of traditional wisdom. To them the world was not a blot, a blank; and to find its meaning was their meat and drink.

Not long before his death the novelist Sir Gilbert Parker

visited a college in California. Dutifully he allowed himself to be conducted about the campus and spent an hour in sparkling conversation in the office of the president. As he was about to leave, with one foot on the running board of the car that had brought him to the academic valley, he almost bashfully remarked: "If you don't mind, I'd like to go for a little while into that chapel again; and I'd rather go alone." So he did, and his hosts waited while he completed his vigil. Was it religion that lured him, or architecture, or the spirit of solitude? Probably all three combining to create an atmosphere of peace. He was like the young lady in Saint Paul's in London who stood rapt and silent before Holman Hunt's painting of Christ the Light of the World. She was not a professedly religious person and in the conventional sense she didn't say her prayers. But she had responded to the appeal of a great religious picture and for a little while she enjoyed the purifying ecstasy of peace.

Cerebral observers have sometimes puzzled over the fondness of numerous persons, not technical musicians, for attending concerts and symphonies. Those admirers of Debussy and Mendelssohn are but slightly influenced by the prestige of the conductor and even less by the social éclat of the occasion; indeed their preference is usually the popular program where Grieg's Norwegian dances alternate with bits from the Wagnerian music dramas, and "Jeanie with the Light Brown Hair" jostles "Where the River Shannon Flows." It is because the snow-bright mountains of music—some of them not very high mountains—bring them peace. Those listeners, if the truth were known, are daily caught in the eddies of various conflicts, within and without. Battered and buffeted by financial worries, domestic disharmonies, frustrated ambitions and hopes deferred, they find in the concert hall a refuge from the world's strident competition and the appalling cross-purposes of their own lives. It would be rash to dismiss them as escapists; it is no more dishonorable to shun contention than to flee from a bad smell. Perhaps they are wiser than their critics; perhaps they have found out that in every war all the belligerents lose. It is neither ignoble nor unmanly to seek after peace and pursue it.

Neither need the self-conscious scholar look down his erudite nose at readers who favor simplified and untechnical books on philosophy. He ought to know that most rational animals find reflection difficult, yet without reflection cannot live satisfying lives. Must not a man's reach exceed his grasp? The mere fact that the word philosophy holds a glamour for some untutored minds should, I think, be immensely fortifying to the academic zoophytes who spend their days building coral reefs of abstract thought. Even on its lowest levels the quest of truth is no crime. It is ungenerous—and unphilosophical—for the man on the mountain top to sneer at the earnest if inexpert climbers far down the slope. The truth that makes us free is not embalmed in a few recondite and esoteric tomes forbidding and forbidden to all but the intellectually elect. For all their shortcomings and limitations, amateur philosophers love the elusive vision of mental peace; they want to find their way, however gropingly, through the dark forest of uncertainty and error, to resolve intellectual conflicts, to set their minds at rest. What have they to do with genera and species and the finespun distinctions of the schools?

Granted, the well-meaning and ill-equipped amateur in the arts, in philosophy, in religion, can easily become an irritation and a bore. He can even, like his betters, be something of a fool. But we are advised on unimpeachable authority to suffer fools gladly. A fellow feeling makes us wondrous kind. In any case, it is a wise folly which enables a man to get out of himself, to minimize his personal troubles, to cover up the scars of earlier experiences. Now, this the imponderables can enable him to do. They bring about the enlargement of personality, not by puffing the individual up, but by inducing him to lose himself, and eventually to find himself, in an ambient vast, rich, beautiful and vitalizing. Beyond the field of battle loom the snow-bright mountains, and on the mountains there is peace.

Present-day pedagogical practice fails, it seems to me, to inculcate this selfless approach to spiritual values. For instance, in the average class in public speaking, the student is urged to be himself, to be "natural" in stance and tone, to get up and say just what he thinks and feels about the labor movement, the Asiatic problem, the future of aviation. In classes devoted to what is grandiosely termed creative writing, he is advised to get his material out of his own life and experience and is warned against writing on themes alien to his personal environment.

Should it not be just the other way around? Is not the learner in any of the arts more likely to achieve mastery of his medium when he forgets himself and loses himself? Writ-

146

ing on "The Art of Successful Singing," Mr. J. Whitcomb Nash insists that the student must school himself to sing self-lessly, forgetting his individual habits, ideas, opinions, that he must resolve the conflict between

> the personal ideas that all of us entertain and the impersonal truth that is at the back of all art. The personal viewpoint that is influenced by our desires and our opinions dams up and shuts off the flow of infinite energies, values and qualities to which all of us are natural heirs. . . . True vocal culture conditions the individual to respond to ideas with appropriate emotion and action, and such responses must be complete and free from personal interference.[1]

The aspiring speaker will enlarge his vocabulary and liberate his soul by losing himself in a vocal interpretation of Portia's plea for mercy, Shelley's "Ozymandias," Kipling's "The Ladies" and Walter de la Mare's "The Listeners." The embryo story writer will develop what gifts he has, not by putting himself and his acquaintances into a factual narrative, but by forgetting his petty and unimportant self in a fictional account of the revolt of the angels, the impressions of a dead man at his own funeral, the amatory adventures of a horned toad or the ambition of a hassock flea to find out what a bishop tastes like. Nothing much matters, really, so long as the student, the amateur, the seeker transcends his narrow and narrowing existence. Art was given us for that; and so were philosophy and religion.

A few years ago there came to the New York stage a flood

[1] *Opera, Concert and Symphony,* John Douglas Cook, editor. October, 1946, San Francisco.

of literal and realistic plays—as literal as the East Side pronunciation of Toity-toid Street, as realistic as real water in a
real bucket. Some of us marveled why we should pay three
dollars and thirty cents to see and hear in a stuffy auditorium
drab and illiterate men and women whom we dodged on the
slippery sidewalk in the next block. Then appeared a revival
of Sheridan's *The Rivals* with Walter Hampden, Mary Bo-
land and Bobby Clarke. The actors used grease paint and
beauty patches, powdered wigs and eighteenth-century cos-
tumes; the settings bore not the slightest resemblance to the
Jersey bus terminal, the language was almost exotic in its
flavorful cadences, and a musical accompaniment enhanced
the artistic illusion. "Why," exclaimed one delighted lady,
"this is just like going to the theater!" That was her way of
saying that for two and a half hours she had been transported
out of her humdrum existence and had breathed the air of
beauty and interior peace.

Men and women who have visited the Rodin museum
and have strolled through the halls of the Louvre will agree
that, whatever their reactions to particular statues and paintings, they succeeded, without effort and even unaware, in
forgetting for the time being their customary occupations
and interests; they may even have shed a few of their cramp-
ing and disfiguring antipathies. It may be true, as art authorities would tell them, that they attempted to cover too much
ground, that they tried to take in too many masterpieces, that
they stood too close to the "Winged Victory," neglected to
squint in orthodox fashion at the statue of Victor Hugo and
made inane remarks apropos of Da Vinci's "Mona Lisa."

Nevertheless, something fine and expanding happened inside them. They walked a world of beauty. They were vouchsafed glimpses of things beyond the horizon of their individual experience. In forgetting themselves they re-created themselves, and they caught something of the high serenity of plastic and pictorial perfection.

The other day an old gentleman waxed reminiscent regarding books he had read in his youth, and unconsciously illustrated Anatole France's definition of criticism—the adventures of the soul among masterpieces. "I cared little for reading and knew nothing of its delights until, at the age of sixteen, I read *The Lady of the Lake*. Before I had finished the first canto—I lived in a sunless house on a noisy city street—I thrilled to the beauty of the Trossachs, breathed the perfume of the heather and identified myself with the huntsman in his discovery of Ellen's Isle. And as I read on I sped with the clansmen through glens and across mountains bearing the Fiery Cross, and reveled in the chain of episodes culminating in the duel of Fitz-James with Roderick Dhu. Best of all, the revelation in the closing verses of Fitz-James's identity came on me with a delicious shock of surprise. When I set down the book—William Rolfe's little green-bound edition, I remember—I felt, as we say nowadays, that I had been places and seen things. Ever since, I have been a reader, especially of poetry." My friend is not the only wayfarer guided by good Sir Walter along the paths of peace that led to the Temple of the Spirit. He would not have gone in that direction had he taken *Tobacco Road*.

What M. Georges Duhamel says of literary classics equally

applies to master achievements in philosophy and music, painting and religion: "We must rediscover them ten and twenty times in order to appreciate their true flavor of novelty, that is to say, of eternity." [2] The peace they bring, infused with supernal wisdom and conditioned by our capacity for balance, moderation and detachment, calls for periodic renewal; the clock of the spirit needs to be wound up. Obviously, plenty of books, profitable and enjoyable though they be, are finished when read once; but other, though fewer, books, De Quincey's literature of power, yield more and more fruition on repeated perusals. The older we grow and the more richly we have lived, the more those books will restore and confirm our sense of values. "The poets are not the bringers of new tidings," writes Mr. Charles Allen Dinsmore, "but are the revealers of the significance of things and of deeds; they bring the obscure to light and say the commonplace with radiant energy. Their glorious platitudes are what men need if they would keep in the paths of true progress. . . . As we read, the veil of the intervening centuries grows thin, and we commune with an immortal face to face; his glory and strength come into us, we see the world through his eyes and add to our consciousness new areas of experience." [3]

The glory and the strength which flow through the imponderables into the human spirit should normally conduce to gracious ease and serene urbanity, a sweetness of temper re-

[2] *In Defense of Letters,* p. 87.
[3] *The Great Poets and the Meaning of Life,* pp. 2-3. © 1937. Published by Houghton Mifflin & Co.

mote from the angularity and cantankerousness of the Cassius-like men who love no plays, who hear no music. The peace which enfolds the Temple of the Spirit is not a passive peace; it overflows into a man's thoughts and works and ways. Into his countenance and the tones of his voice. It teaches him, as Mr. E. R. Clinchy would say, to agree to disagree agreeably. How, then, account for the flagrantly familiar fact that partisans of the imponderables so frequently flare into fighting moods? Why is it that Berlioz is a fighting word, that mention of Whitman provokes the smile that mocks itself, that sundry philosophers see red when they encounter the name of Pascal or Kant, Spencer or Dr. John Dewey, that biting and scratching human animals find a field day in religious discussions and that the wars of religion are among the gravest scandals throughout the Christian centuries? Why is it that men dedicated to the things that make for peace are so often unseemly passions' slaves?

Mainly, I suspect, because those troubled spirits *are* partisans. They have not allowed the imponderables to get into the blood stream of their souls. Theirs, as Epictetus explains, are "the perturbations of men who cherish externals." They mistake the school for the idea, the method for the principle, the grammar for the language, the symbol for the reality, the sect for supernatural wisdom, the tree of knowledge for the tree of life. Hence, knowledge may come but wisdom lingers. Music, art and literature, especially philosophy and religion, can drive men asunder, though their essential function is to draw men together. Those human thorn-trees have not found themselves because they have not dared to lose themselves;

151

their bumptious loyalties are but pretexts for self-seeking and self-assertion. They have not developed detachment, humility and reverence; they have not tasted the sweets of solitude and glimpsed the majesty of silence. "You can never play that passage properly," Toscanini said at rehearsal to one of his professional musicians; "you haven't a sufficiently generous soul." Magnanimity, spiritual greatness, is both a prerequisite and a consequence of interior peace.

Let the partisans and the politicians, the sectarians and the schismatics lift their eyes unto the hills. Let them cease quarreling over the comparative altitudes of petty peaks and behold the serrated ranges steadily and whole. Let them forget the tarantulas and the rattlesnakes on the mountainsides, the nightshade and the poison oak, the dead timber and the withered blooms and the pollen to which they are allergic. Only then will they perceive that the imponderables are not bones for ill-bred dogs to fight over, but a haven of security and serenity wherein sage and civilized men may live free and fruitful lives.

To a stone house high on the shore of a sequestered lake where a few peace-loving people have built their homes, there dashes now and then an impetuous man of desires. A dream possesses him. He would like to abandon his professional routine in the big city forty miles away, and live his life and write his books where the breeze from the near-by ocean mingles its salinity with the pungent mountain odors and where at nightfall the homing blackbirds chatter in the reeds. This poet's vision takes a form peculiar to himself. He is not just another solitude-hungry soul seeking seclusion. His dreams make sense, really, for there is an idea in it and a wealth of symbolism. On the low rounded island in the middle of the lake he would erect a chapel, a miniature Mont-Saint-Michel; and for himself he would pre-empt the office of sacristan, dwelling obscure in the shadow of the holy house and in view of the lordly western mountains. Some day he may literally realize his dream.

But, figuratively, we can all realize his dream. Within sight of the peace-bringing mountains we can erect our Temple of the Spirit.

X THE PERFECT LAW

He who journeys toward the Temple of the Spirit is sooner or later harried by conflicts between his own impulses and intuitions on the one hand, and by the advices and admonitions of previous pilgrims on the other. The road signs and traffic signals bemuse him. He wonders if the longest way around is ever the shortest cut, if a forced march is more rewarding than a desultory stroll, if joining a guarded caravan is preferable to setting forth unarmed and alone. In his innocent eagerness he doubts that sundry time-tested techniques are not invalidated by the passing of the years.

His sane procedure, obviously, is to seek a happy mean between undiscriminating obedience to the dicta of the masters and the self-defeating egotism which exalts his own impressions and preferences into the supreme criterion of values. He is wise when he avoids the callow provincialism which assumes that the best that has been thought and known and accomplished is found only in one epoch or in the stream of but one cultural tradition; he is equally wise when he gives heed to the words of Mr. W. Macneile Dixon:

> To its eternal honor Christianity has stood steadfastly for the sanctity of the individual. To imprison the human spirit is the

unpardonable sin, the attempt to make men automata, to force them into the same mould. No means will ever be found to induce human beings finally to surrender themselves, either body or soul, to a dictated felicity, to satisfactions chosen for them, whatever vulgar Caesars rule the world. And upon this rock all forms of regimentation, of standardized existence will eventually shipwreck. Every type of compulsion is hateful, always has been, and always will be hateful, as long as men are men.[1]

Yet the neophyte knows, if he knows anything at all about human psychology and human history, that osseous leaders, motivated by what might be called the higher expediency, have made Christianity a pretext for submerging and repressing the individual, and that ever so many individuals in ever so many eras have yielded themselves, reluctantly or ardently, to one or another form of intellectual and social serfdom. Hopeful of attaining to certitude, security or peace, they have submitted to regimentation, welcomed a standardized existence, embraced a dictated felicity. Esau was not the only man to sell his birthright for a mess of pottage—or for pie in the sky. True, the vulgar Caesars seldom rule for long; but they enjoy recurring reincarnations.

Not every man is a conformist, and not every man is a rebel. Not all conformity is slavery, and not all rebellion is heroic. In both attitudes there are degrees of virtue and vice. Slavery to fashions in clothing is less tragic than slavery to fashions in thought; rebellion against theories is less tragic than rebellion against truth. Rebellion for the sake of rebel-

[1] *The Human Situation,* p. 190.

lion is as childish and unworthy as conformity for the sake
of conformity. There needs must be liberty and there needs
must be law, and the conflicts between them are resolved
in the perfect law of liberty.

Unfortunately, most mortals, rebels and conformists alike,
are not sufficiently farseeing and magnanimous to resolve
such conflicts. It is easier to go it blind, to give unquestion-
ing loyalty to an opinion or a tradition, a manifesto or a myth.
Whether in diehard or insurrectionist, the closed mind is
the devil's garden. As pathological profiles of the closed
mind in action I submit the following psychographs of two
men whom I name Lionel and Luke. Neither of them, of
course, is so extreme as here depicted. I am not writing their
biographies and I deliberately suppress most of their endearing traits. The result is caricature; but caricature, as Hogarth
two hundred years ago and Lichty and Low in our own day
demonstrate, has its moral and educational uses. In this case
it may induce Luke and Lionel to laugh at each other, and
may prompt us who laugh at both of them to search our
own hearts.

Lionel is a violinist and, considering his comparative youth,
a capable musician. He has technique and a soul. He has
learned to face difficulties and solve problems, to submit his
judgment to the decisions of a conductor, to unite himself
with the other members of the orchestra in which he so
brilliantly performs.

Outside of his professional interests, however, Lionel is
an outspoken and almost an anarchistic libertarian. His library bulges with books that assail civil government, dismiss

religion as an outworn superstition, exalt self-expression into the supreme virtue. He drives his car and parks it according to the whim of the moment, and has paid out enough money in traffic courts to maintain a small family in modest affluence. He simply does not believe in law, and formulates his own conceptions of order. "If I feel like doing a thing," he asks, "why shouldn't I do it?" Grasping at every privilege, he ignores corresponding responsibilities. He is utterly and unashamedly selfish. Consciously and complacently he is a modern—holding that the wisdom of the past should be discarded as so much rubbish. You can hear his mind slam shut at mention of the *philosophia perennis.* To him all statesmen are scoundrels, all saints are neurotics, all thinkers—save, of course, the few with whom he deigns to agree—are insufferable blockheads. He is convinced that he knows everything worth knowing.

Luke is a lecturer, a scholar and an occasional writer on weighty topics. Though old enough and experienced enough to do his own thinking and frame his own philosophy of life, he cleaves unquestioningly and unwaveringly to the party line—in politics, in pedagogy, in general outlook. One of his less conventional colleagues once said of Luke that he would not use his handkerchief without consulting a father confessor or a psychiatrist. Novelty, originality, independence are words he abhors as of satanic origin. Lionel's favorite volumes Luke would sweepingly condemn as superficial and heretical. He reads his mail with pencil poised, ready to spear a split infinitive or slay a terminal preposition. New books he approaches in the attitude of a rigorous schoolmaster correcting themes written by students who have an altogether too good conceit of themselves. An epigram of Wilde's, a paradox of Chesterton's he damns as an affront to formal logic. He deplores Abbé Dimnet as an unsystematic thinker. His thinning hair is trimmed every two weeks and his mind keeps office hours. His notion of scholarship is a continuous literal reproduction of what venerated predecessors have written and taught. *Magister dixit* is to Luke a magic formula that settles everything from the immortality of the soul to the immorality of the cinema.

Lionel's individualism hampers his quest of freedom. He puts too much emphasis on liberty, too little emphasis on law. He expects all his trees to attain their full growth overnight, and disdains the distasteful labor of preparing the soil, carting manure and spraying parasites. He completely misses the social implications of the imponderables and writes poems that nobody else can understand, paints pictures that look like scrambled jigsaw puzzles and professes to find God—if there be a God—in forest shade and desert glare rather than in assemblies of the faithful.

Luke, on the contrary, puts too much emphasis on law and too little emphasis on liberty. He is unduly impressed with the potential dangers of freedom, not at all with its vital possibilities. He is a Boileau in poetry, a Del Sarto in art, a Brunetière in criticism. His considerable scholarship becomes a network of intellectual and spiritual restrictions. His mental landscape is crisscrossed with hedges and fences, and he never leaps over any of them.

Lionel and Luke represent two extreme and sharply con-

159

flicting attitudes toward the perfect law of liberty. Lionel is thoracic in temperament, Luke is motor, and never the twain shall meet. It is a fascinating fancy to conjecture what two splendid men they might be were some super-scientist to mix their personalities, stir thoroughly and pour the psychic decoction into appropriate bodily frames. Because of his exclusive addiction to personal license and his bitter contempt of rules and walls and fences, Lionel is missing a lot of fun, contracting spiritual myopia and impeding his progress toward the Temple of the Spirit. And Luke, because of his frenzied formalism and his irrational suspicion of independence is wearing other men's cast-off garments, stifling the aspirations of his soul and binding his intellect as disastrously as Chinese ladies used to bind their feet. Lionel is like fruit grown rotten before it is ripe, Luke like fruit frostbitten and desiccated on the tree.

The seventeenth-century Jesuit, Balthasar Gracian, astute, urbane and worldly-wise, was familiar with the Lionel and Luke mentalities. Of Lionel's penchant for judging everything by exclusively individual standards Gracian observes: "He is an insufferable ass who would regulate everything according to his own ideas. Excellences do not depend on a single man's pleasure. . . . You should aim to be independent of any one choice, of any one fashion, of any one country." And as for Luke's habit of heresy hunting in several countrysides, the Spanish thinker observes: "There is nothing that has no good in it, especially in books, as giving food for thought. But many readers have such a sense of smell that amid a thousand excellences they fix upon a solitary defect, and single it out for blame as if they were scavengers of men's minds and hearts. So they draw up a balance sheet of defects, which does more credit to their bad taste than to their intelligence. They lead a sad life, nourishing themselves on bitterness and battening on garbage." [2]

In learning to read a water meter or play the piano, to pilot an airplane or paint a picture, the beginner obviously must sit at the feet of the masters. He need not sit there through all his days, but even if called to be a rebel it will help him to know precisely what or whom he is rebelling against. However much he may dislike the word, he must be a conformist in his period of pupilage. Certain techniques, practices, procedures have to be learned, even if later on some or all of them are to be discarded. Docility, submissiveness is a prerequisite in all the arts, including the art of living. Table etiquette and voice placement, ballet dancing and the habit of reflection are not gifts bestowed at birth. They are acquisitions, often painfully and laboriously secured. There is, of course, such a thing as native capacity for this or that art, but such talent calls for an initial period of formal development. All beginners need to practice their scales. The poet is born *and* made. So is the teacher, the violinist, the priest and the prophet. Each is a Jacob submitting to the exactions of a Laban in order eventually to possess his Rachel.

The Lionels of this world are frequently pushed into the

[2] *Oráculo Manual*, translated by Joseph Jacobs under the title, *The Art of Worldly Wisdom* (New York: Macmillan Company), 1944, pp. 56-57, 81. © Macmillan & Co., Ltd.

path of unwisdom by well-meaning but profoundly unrealistic parents. "I don't want my little Oswald to have any inhibitions," declares the doting mother, immersed in woolly thinking and that little learning which is a dangerous thing. It does not occur to the good woman that her little Oswald decidedly needs a few inhibitions, and that in encouraging him to do and say what he pleases, to have tantrums and order her about like an oriental potentate, she is giving him a pathetically imperfect preparation for life. It will do little Oswald no harm to grasp the idea that cows and goats do not exist for the sole purpose of supplying his milk, that visitors are not supposed to be walked over and like it, that tableware and bric-a-brac serve a purpose other than to be knocked about at his imperial whim. Of books on child training there is no end, but their theories, often admirable, we seldom carry into fruitful practice; we do a better job with our puppies and our ponies.

The pianist and teacher, Miss Rosalyn Tureck, while thinking specifically of the student of music, offers a principle that applies to the neophyte in all the arts:

> If we did not live in a cultivated and fairly civilized world, there would be no need of teaching. It becomes necessary, however, at that point where existence departs from the instinctive state. A great talent will know much instinctively, but, if that innate knowledge is to be used or expressed with the purpose of being understood, it needs cultivation in order to be clearly projected. There is no possibility of expression without some sort of language, and language is not a natural phenomenon: it is man-made, artificial and cultivated. Teaching is needed where cultivation appears.

With the talented student, the distinction must be made be-tween his own innate perceptions and his needs in the culti-vated language and forms. If this is clearly understood, the field of teaching becomes valid, vast and fruitful. One of the greatest dangers is the confusion of the two types of knowledge, the innate and the cultured. The most difficult problem is illuminat-ing learnable knowledge without distorting and blocking the expression of the inner vision.[3]

Outside his strictly professional interests, Lionel would violently dissent from Miss Tureck's statement, and Luke would fervently approve it; but Luke would be less in agree-ment with her further contention that one objective of the teacher's art is to give "the student freedom from the need of teaching," that the good teacher "works to give up stu-dents rather than to keep them." Luke, in short, believes in lifelong tutelage in art, philosophy, religion; Lionel believes that tutelage, even for the novice, is an imposition and a form of slavery. Many individuals are like Lionel, and many in-stitutions are like Luke. Either extreme distorts and violates the perfect law of liberty. Liberty! What crimes—and not only in politics—have been committed in thy name!

A popular cartoon represents a mother ostrich exhorting her offspring still imprisoned in the egg: "There *is* no door, I tell you! You'll have to find your own way out." We have all been baby ostriches. Confined in the shell of custom and prejudice, of untested formulas and unscrutinized be-liefs, we indeed have to find our own way out. The Lionels

[3] Questioning the Teacher's Rank," *Opera, Concert and Symphony,* John Douglas Cook, editor, November, 1946.

start pecking at the shell too early; the Lukes never start pecking at all.

Independence is normally achieved when, for one thing, we rid ourselves of *logophobia*, the irrational fear of words. Every epoch in history, every stage of personal development, every school and coterie has its own little dictionary of deprecation, lists of words to be used as missiles to terrify the timid and hold the loyal in line: bourgeois, old-fashioned, modernist, fascist, heretic, reactionary, unscholarly, superficial, unscientific, authoritarian, radical and the rest. The pilgrim striving toward the Temple of the Spirit, the seeker after the imponderables, must expect to be pelted with epithets, to be ridiculed or reprobated by men who imagine that calling names is the most pragmatic form of argument. And yet, as Thomas à Kempis so shrewdly observed, "What are words but words?" Most of the words the thin-skinned shrink from are susceptible of comforting definition; to be a conservative, for example, is to hold fast that which is good, to be a radical is to get to the roots of ideas and institutions. Some unwise things have been written anent the science of semantics, but the all too transient vogue of the movement has at least brought thinking men and women to see that words are little more than what we choose to make them, that when traced back to their origins many opprobrious epithets lose their sting and even acquire halos.

Even as words, popular and unpopular, should be looked squarely in the face, so should theories and ideas that our own age unconsciously and uncritically accepts as permanent wisdom and eternal truth. Is it a fact that things every day in every way are getting better and better? Does it follow that a people who use washing machines are more cultivated and enlightened than a people who use washtubs or smooth stones beside a river? Is self-expression intrinsically more important and desirable than self-repression; is not breathing in as necessary as breathing out? Are we justified in accepting a movie star as an authority on domestic relations, a clergyman as an expert on dramatic art, a society leader as a judge of literature, a business tycoon as a theologian, a newspaper columnist as an arbiter of disputes on every subject from dogma to dysentery, from politics to pedagogy?

Lionel talks at great length about originality in thought and life, but to him originality means being different at all costs, startling and shocking his stodgy fellow citizens. Granted that, as Swift said, the world needs to be vexed; granted that many otherwise worthy men need to be blasted out of their ruts and their squirrel cages. But Lionel in his intemperate devotion to originality is in a rather deep rut of his own; and his frequent and prolonged fulminations against decorum, tradition and conventionality resemble the shrill chattering of a squirrel protesting against the bars that enclose—and protect—him.

Luke, on the other hand, views any manifestation of originality with distrust and hostility. Did not Aristotle say everything in philosophy? Have there been any great painters since the Renaissance? Is not Frank Lloyd Wright an architectural mountebank and Eugene O'Neill a theatrical buffoon? Luke dissents violently from the belief that in many fields of thought every age requires a fresh re-statement of principles and that terminology, like trousers, can burst at the seams. He holds no brief for new wine in old bottles; to him old bottles are precious relics, and he honestly believes there is no such product as new wine.

In their sharply opposing attitudes toward originality Lionel errs through excess and Luke through defect. Both of them think and talk too much about it. Originality is like bodily health and spiritual vigor—most in evidence when we are unconscious of possessing them. Originality is neither to be deliberately cultivated nor inquisitorially burned at the stake. It is a by-product of profound thought and zestful living; and the way to acquire it is through intelligent imitation of the best exemplars in philosophy, art and religion—great minds and established masterpieces.

Lionel sees red at mention of imitation, and Luke misconceives its nature and purpose. For Lionel regards imitation as a form of serfdom, and Luke as thinking and doing the same old things in the same old way. Lionel would do well to remember the saying of Georges Duhamel that imitation is "humiliating only for minds that are ill-formed or presumptuous"; but Luke has no reason to read those words with complacency. The path to liberty does indeed lead through the valley of bondage, but it does not end there. A philosopher whom Luke commendably admires wrote that imitation consists, not in playing copy-cat to greatness, but in following greatness in its *principles of operation*. So did La Bruyère follow Theophrastus, so did Franklin and Stevenson learn to write English prose, so was Keats inspired by Chapman's "sea-shouldering whales," so was Berlioz liberated from his youthful callowness when he heard Habeneck play Beethoven. Perhaps Goethe had something for both Luke and Lionel to meditate upon: "To say a thing as quietly as though nobody else had ever said it, that is originality." Lionel would find difficulty in saying anything quietly; Luke would be fearful of saying anything that somebody else had not already said.

The Lionels may be a nuisance and an irritation, but seldom are there too many of them. It is the Lukes who constitute the majority of mortals and who in the realm of the imponderables usually inherit the earth. For the most part, men do not really wish for spiritual freedom; many are afraid of it. They are reluctant to accept the discipline of thought, of art; it is easier to give untempered allegiance to a school, a clique, a fashion, to repeat parrotwise the dicta of leaders, many of whom are blind guides to the blind. Not all of the self-styled intelligentsia are intelligent. To spiritual liberty, many are called but few are chosen—because they do not choose to accept the perfect law of liberty. Theirs is what William James called the Gray Plastic Temperament. Their devotion, often intense, to literature and the arts, to philosophy and religion, is conscientious and literal, rarely colorful and dynamic. They are like Tibetan monks spinning prayer wheels. They make dependable lodge members, and their leaders prefer to have them that way. The powers that be— good osseous men—invariably bless the Lukes and damn the Lionels—at least until the Lionels, who often die young, are decently and definitely interred.

In a poetic sense the child is father of the man, but in no sense is the child master of the man. "When I was a child," wrote Saint Paul, "I spoke as a child, I understood as a child, I thought as a child; but when I became a man I put away childish things." That is the apostle's way of saying that through law he had won to liberty, that the development of his physical powers was paralleled by changes in his inner life. He had outgrown his childhood conceptions as he had outgrown his baby shoes. Change is a law—though not the only law—of constructive and fruitful living. To Lionel, change is excellent for its own sake; to Luke, change is an indication of disloyalty and inconsistency. Luke ignores the fact that every kind of growth involves some kind of change, that a man is not disloyal when in the light of learning, experience and insight he discards outworn ideas, systems, allegiances, the better to live on a higher plane of being. Neither is a man inconsistent when he strives to follow the truth whithersoever it leads him. "The high soul takes the high road," the road often unseen by the system-shackled soul.

Untenable, however, is Lionel's assumption—an assumption gratuitously accepted by so many of his contemporaries —that any change is a change for the better. "Off with the old, on with the new" is a motto to be taken with a considerable grain of salt. That facile faith in the blessedness of change overlooks the fact that in physical and spiritual processes devolution is as frequent as evolution. Perhaps a wiser formula would be: Change your mind as often as you like, but see to it that each change brings you to a higher level

of character and outlook. Applicable to all the imponderables are the admonitions of the late Ellen Glasgow:

> To the scholar and the critic I would say simply: Keep an
> open mind, but hold fast to the standard of excellence—for an
> open mind without standards may become little more than a
> rubbish heap. . . . For in an epoch of general disintegration,
> when the lowest common denominator is the popular hero, it
> takes finer courage to commend excellence than to applaud
> mediocrity. And it takes more than courage—it takes irresistible
> daring—to cherish and defend that benign, if discredited
> virtue, good taste.[4]

In Mr. Marquand's *B. F.'s Daughter,* Tom Brett, who is
something of a Lionel, complains that tolerance so rarely
characterizes the open mind; it should, but it doesn't. Too
often the open mind exemplifies liberty without law—which
means uncontrolled license—and, as Ellen Glasgow points
out, the limited freedom of the rubbish heap and the sewer.
As for tolerance, that is an inadequate word for a noble idea
—inadequate because any man conscious of his dignity as a
human being dislikes and resents being tolerated. At its best,
tolerance means the art and the act of a reasonable patience,
founded on humility and wisdom, which respects the nature,
the needs and the preferences of others. Intolerant are both
the Lukes and the Lionels of this tragi-comic world.

Underlying Ellen Glasgow's timely utterance is the solid
conviction that law connotes liberty and liberty connotes
law. One would be meaningless without the other. Rulers

[4] From "Elder and Younger Brother" in *Saturday Review of Literature,*
© January 23, 1937.

become tyrants, poets write gibberish, philosophers talk nonsense and holy men fall into fanaticism because they fail to see that, basically, liberty *is* law and law *is* liberty. Freedom bestows a patent of nobility, but *noblesse oblige;* as Saint Augustine put it, "Love, and do what you will." Law implies the existence of a freedom, a surging force, a beautiful wild horse which needs to be bridled, but not sent to the boneyard.

Neither law alone nor liberty alone can erect the Temple of the Spirit. Spiritual architecture has its laws, its precedents, its time-tested and labor-saving traditions; but if the architect is to build something other than a lifeless and uninspired replica of outmoded structures, he must have his freedoms, his spirit of adventure, his freshened faiths and deepened insights. In the creation and the appreciation of the imponderables we need, as Havelock Ellis wrote, "the utmost freedom and the utmost restraint." Luke will tremble at the prospect of freedom, and Lionel will scoff at the suggestion of restraint, yet in the happy and harmonious equilibrium of those centripetal and centrifugal forces of the human soul can be found the formula whereby the builder builds not in vain. "For ye have been called unto liberty; only use not liberty for an occasion to the flesh."

The ultimate of law and the ultimate of liberty are adumbrated by the late Lecomte du Noüy in his thoughtful and enlarging book, *Human Destiny.* Correlating the knowledge of thinker and artist, reconciling the objectives of scientist and saint, he presents a long-range vista of the possibilities of man's further development and the fulfillment of man's highest aspirations. He offers scholarly and reverent illustration of Mr. Dooley's casual remark that "the Christians need more science and the scientists need more Christianity." It is Du Noüy's well-documented conviction that the ascent of man has been slowly but steadily in the direction of the imponderables, that the so-called lord of creation will eventually justify his germinal nobility. But today, more than in earlier periods of history, advance toward the far-off divine event depends upon the intelligent and unselfish exercise of man's free will. The human race can destroy itself or can re-make itself in the image and likeness of God.

We need not stress the possibilities of man's racial suicide. The lust for power, the servile state, the deification of greed, the negation of individual dignity, the acceptance of trivial and corrupting standards in life and in art, the ignoring or denigration of spiritual values all tend to frustration, to impotence, to despair. Recurrent wars which nobody wins and the invention of weapons of destruction which nobody can wisely use are evidence that man can stultify himself. The peril is grave, the prospect terrifying. Sterile are politics without prayer and crusades without the Cross.

But there are other and heartening possibilities. Animal but more than animal, earth-dwelling but not earth-bound, the individual man can lift up his mind and his heart. Existing in the swirl of competition and class struggle, his nostrils stung by the exhaust of motor cars and his ears dulled by the clangor of machinery, man can, if he will, remember that the ponderable world which is his monetary home is surrounded by the infinite world of the imponderables. He need not and should not seek permanent escape from the problems and perplexities of daily life, for that, as Mr. C. S. Lewis has aptly said, is to run away from horses rather than learning to ride them. But he can learn to ride them better, and be happier in the saddle, if his gallop—or even his canter—leads him to the noblest thought, the highest artistry and the deepest religious philosophy which the human mind has achieved.

One evening a visitor in Denver was crossing the Capitol Park in the direction of turbulent Colfax Avenue. A ground fog obscured his view of the park statuary and the steps of the state house, and only the rumble of streetcars, the tooting of auto horns and the rumorous tides of traffic told of the tumult of city works and ways. He lifted his eyes and saw above the shrouding fog the spires of a cathedral pointing to the sky. Their bases were invisible, and had he been literal-minded and ignorant he might have concluded that they had no tangible support, no essential contact with the earth above which they seemed to hover, that they were nothing more than unusual and exaggerated toy balloons. But reason and experience assured him that white stone towers don't go floating around in space, that they must surmount a massive building at the moment unseen but which must be a haven of holiness and beauty, silence and peace.

So it is with those of us who cherish the imponderables. We may be called idealists, but we are not chasing toy balloons; we may be called visionaries, but even in an atmosphere menacing and dark we see at least the spires of the Temple of the Spirit. Beneath our feet the material earth is tangible and real, but within the range of our vision those spires loom, intangible but even more vitally real. They symbolize the substance of things hoped for, the evidence of things that in their wholeness and perfection elude our feeble gaze. There lies our hope—for man and for men.

INDEX

INDEX